Teachers' Manual

by Diana Kleyn

To be used alongside either:
* Bible Questions and Answers for Children
by Carine Mackenzie
or
* My First Book of Questions and Answers
by Carine Mackenzie

Teachers' Manual

Catechism

by Carine MacKenzie

Teachers' Manual

by Diana Kleyn

**Using the
King James Version**

© Copyright 2001 Christian Focus Publications ISBN: 1-85792-701-X
Published by Christian Focus Publications Ltd, Geanies House, Fearn,
Tain, Ross-shire, IV20 1TW, Scotland, Great Britain.
www.christianfocus.com, email:info@christianfocus.com
Catechism text by Carine Mackenzie
Manual text by Diana Kleyn
Cover design by Alister Macinnes
Printed and bound in Great Britain by Guernsey Press

Bible Questions and Answers Teachers' Manual
by Diana Kleyn

This has been developed for use alongside *Bible Questions and Answers* by Carine Mackenzie

The format of the manual is as follows:

- **Catechism Questions**

- **Scripture Proofs**

- **Lesson Objectives**

- **Lesson and explanation
  Teaching aids and ideas**

- **Discussion questions and application**

The Bible is God's Word to humanity, and within its pages is contained everything we need to know to be reconciled to God and live in a way that pleases him. It is vital that children are taught accurately from God's Word and that sound Christian doctrine and truth is explained to them at an early age. This is the ethos behind this catechism and teachers' manual. It is our prayer that lives will be changed as a result and that God will indeed be glorified.

Introduction

This manual has been written as an instructional aid to the *Children's Catechism: Bible Questions and Answers* by Carine Mackenzie. The questions are grouped into lessons. Since the children you will be teaching are quite young, only one or two questions, or occasionally three, are included in each lesson so that the memory work does not become overwhelming. Also, too many different concepts in one lesson tend to confuse children. The suggested Bible stories are meant to enhance the doctrinal truths in the questions.

Each lesson has one or more suggested Bible stories. A story might be suggested more than once, in connection with more than one lesson. On page 141 you will find a list of the stories suggested, which will help you map out your choice of Bible stories. This way you will avoid using the same story more than once or twice.

Sometimes additional texts are provided. These can be used for your own reference, or as an alternative or extra memory verse for the children. Encourage the children to try to memorize the scripture passages. They might not be able to remember them perfectly, but it will be beneficial for them to read and study these scripture passages. Keep in mind that some children learn easily, while others struggle, sometimes working longer and harder at their memory work than the quick learners. While memory work is important, especially memorizing scripture, it is equally important that the children understand what they have learned.

At the end of each lesson you will find some questions. These can be used by you as a teacher to apply the lessons spiritually. The children do not necessarily have to answer you verbally, but do urge the children to think seriously about these questions during the week. Point them to the Lord Jesus Christ. Your task as a Sunday School teacher is, by the power of the Holy Spirit, to lead the children to the Saviour.

Prepare yourself for each lesson by praying for yourself and for the children, asking the Lord to help you bring His Word to them. Ask the Holy Spirit to speak to the heart of each child. May God richly bless you as you labour in His kingdom.

Contents

Salvation

Jesus as Prophet, Priest and King

The Ten Commandments

The First Commandment

The Second Commandment

GOD (Questions 1-18)

Lesson One

**1. *Who made you?*
God.**

"So God created man in his own image, in the image of God created he him; male and female created he them" (Genesis 1:27).

**2. Why did God make you?
To glorify him and enjoy him.**

"Whether therefore ye eat, or drink, or whatsoever ye do, do all to the glory of God" (1 Corinthians 10:31).

<u>Objective</u>: To teach the children that God made man to glorify him.

Because Questions 3 and 4 are about the creation, the children may be confused if you tell them the story of man's creation at this point. You have several options. You could do all four questions in a lesson, but that may be too much to cover at once. You could stretch out the story of the creation over several lessons, beginning with this lesson, in which case the questions will not fit the story perfectly.

Another option is to tell a story which addresses the second question in this lesson a bit more directly than the first. For instance, if you choose to tell the parable of the man and his two sons (Matthew 21:28-32), you can talk about the difference between the two boys. When we disobey God, we are not doing or being what he has created us to be. When we are obedient, then God is pleased. Remember to address the fact that the son who eventually obeyed his father was rebellious at first, just as we all are by nature. We must ask the Lord for a heart that is willing to obey him.

The story of the houses on the rock and on the sand (Matthew 7:24-29; Luke 6:46-49) is a bit more abstract, but also fits this lesson. One house was a good house, the other was not. We must be like the good house, safely built on the rock, which, of course, is Jesus Christ.

Questions:
1. Do you wish to honour and glorify God by obeying him?
2. Are you sad when you have been disobedient? What should you do after you have sinned?

Lesson Two

3. What else did God make?
God made all things.

"And God saw every thing that he had made, and, behold, it was very good" (Genesis 1:31a).

4. Why did God make all things?
For his own glory.

"Thou art worthy, O Lord, to receive glory and honour and power: for thou hast created all things, and for thy pleasure they are and were created" (Revelation 4:11).

<u>Objective</u>: To teach the children that God made all things for his own glory.

The most obvious choice of story for this lesson is the creation (Genesis 1). It may be beneficial to give the children a worksheet about the six days of creation to fill in or colour. If you don't have enough time, or feel it is too much for one lesson, spread the questions over two teaching sessions. Be less concerned about the children memorizing exactly what happened on each day, than on the wonder of creation. Stop and marvel at the beauty of God's creation! Bring in some "simple" things: a pretty rock, some moss, a leaf, a flower, a caterpillar, a moth, etc. Point out the intricate design in each creation. Our God is an amazing God! You can easily tie in the simple gospel message: this great God is able to save you.

Questions:
1. Can you think of things that God made, that no one else is able to make?
2. Have you ever been amazed at God's power and at the many beautiful things he made?

Lesson Three

5. Where does God teach us to praise and enjoy him?
In his Word, the Bible.

"Search the scriptures; for in them ye think ye have eternal life: and they are they which testify of me" (John 5:39).

6. Who wrote the Bible?
Holy men who were taught by the Holy Spirit.

"All scripture is given by inspiration of God, and is profitable for doctrine, for reproof, for correction, for instruction in righteousness" (2 Timothy 3:16).

<u>Objective</u>: To teach the children that God instructs us in His inspired Word to praise Him.

You can start the lesson by talking about the inspiration of the scriptures. There are several instances in the Bible where it specifically says that God told a person to write down His words: Jeremiah (36:2); Habakkuk (2:2); John (Revelation 1:3; 14:13). You may want to choose one of these men and tell about their lives. Read and discuss some of the passages they wrote by the inspiration of the Holy Spirit, specifically ones that teach us to praise and enjoy God. (Keep it simple, though!)

If this seems too difficult for the children you are teaching, do something simpler. Find some easy passages in the Bible, write them on a large piece of paper, or on a worksheet, and discuss them.

For example: *"Love one another" (John 15:12);* *"Be ye kind one to another, tenderhearted, forgiving one another" (Ephesians 4:32);* *"I delight to do thy will, O my God: yea, thy law is within my heart" (Psalm 40:8),* etc. Ask the children how these texts are helpful to us.

The entire Bible is profitable, says 2 Timothy 3:16. Stress the value of private devotions, and of asking the Holy Spirit (and Mom or Dad!) to help us understand God's Word. In the pages of the Bible, we find the way to God through Jesus Christ (John 5:39).

There are many different things you could bring out in this lesson, but don't make it too difficult for the little children. The main goal is to teach them to treasure God's Word, which is God's "letter" to us, telling us the way to be saved.

Questions:
1. Do you love God?
2. Do you love his Word?
3. Why should we love God and his Word?

Lesson Four

7. What is God?
God is a spirit.

"God is a Spirit: and they that worship him must worship him in spirit and in truth" (John 4:24).

8. What is a spirit?
An invisible being who does not have a body like us.

"Who is the image of the invisible God, the firstborn of every creature" (Colossians 1:15).

Objective: To teach the children that God is a Spirit.

Do not expect the children to fully understand what a spirit is, because young children are very "concrete", i.e., they are not developmentally capable of grasping abstract concepts such as time, money, maps, etc. You can tell them that the Lord Jesus compared the Holy Spirit to the wind in John 3:8. We can see the effect the wind has, but the wind itself is not visible. Depending on how you want to approach this lesson, there are several stories you could tell. The plagues of Egypt (Exodus 7 - 12) showed God's existence, even though He could not be seen. The pillar of the cloud (Exodus 13:21) was not God Himself, but a sign of His presence, as was the ark of the covenant. The Israelites made a golden calf (Exodus 32) because they were tired of waiting for Moses, and could not see God. They thought about all the idols of the Egyptians, and followed the example of the heathens.

Also, the many battles that God fought for His people Israel are examples of His invisible presence. The walls of Jericho fell at God's command (Joshua 6). A less familiar story is David's conquest of the Philistines with God's help. David asked the Lord for help, and God said that when David would hear a sound in the tops of the mulberry trees, he was to go to meet the Philistines, "for then shall the LORD go out before thee, to smite the host of the Philistines" (2 Samuel 5:24b; parallel passage in 1 Chronicles 14:15).

Some New Testament examples would be the story of Paul being healed after being stoned and left for dead (Acts 14:19, 20), as well as the snake bite that did not injure Paul (Acts 28:3-6). There are countless other stories you could use. The main idea for this lesson is that we cannot see God because He is an invisible being. We know He exists because of what He does.

Questions:
1. Do you believe that God is real? How do you know he is real?
2. Does that make you happy?

Lesson Five

9. Where is God?
God is everywhere.

"Canst thou by searching find out God? canst thou find out the Almighty unto perfection?" (Job 11:7).

Objective: To teach the children that God is *omnipresent* (everywhere).

To introduce this mind-boggling concept, you could ask the children what the birds are doing right now. And how about the bugs and the plants? What about all the dogs and cats and cows and sheep? Then what about all the people in the world? Ask the children if they think they could keep track of what every animal and person is doing all the time. Tell them that this is what God does all the time. He is everywhere, and he controls everything.

A simple story that illustrates this is Jesus healing the centurion's servant (Matthew 8). Jesus had only to speak a word and the servant was healed in his home.

A beautiful thought to send the children home with, is Jesus' words in Matthew 10:29-31: "Are not two sparrows sold for a farthing? and one of them shall not fall on the ground without your Father. But the very hairs of your head are all numbered. Fear ye not therefore, ye are of more value than many sparrows."

Questions:
1. Are you glad that God is everywhere?
2. Why is it good that God is everywhere?

Lesson Six

10. Did God have a beginning?
No. He has always existed.

"Before the mountains were brought forth, or ever thou hadst formed the earth and the world, even from everlasting to everlasting, thou art God" (Psalm 90:2).

11. Will he have an end?
No. He will always exist.

"But thou art the same, and thy years shall have no end" (Psalm 102:27).

Objective: To teach the children that God is eternal.

Humans will never be able to understand this concept. How can a person have no beginning or no end? It is something we cannot fathom, but must simply believe.

If you want to bring in a visual aid, you could bring in a ball of yarn. Perhaps you will want to let the children unwind the yarn. It will be a very long string, but there *will* be a beginning and an end. Have the children try to imagine a string that goes on for ever and ever. We cannot imagine this!

God is an eternal Spirit, with no beginning, and no end. He was always there and always will be.

I don't think there is an actual story in the Bible that displays God's eternal existence, since the stories are set in time. You could tell the story of the Jews challenging Jesus' Godhead. Jesus' answer to them was, "Verily, verily, I say unto you, Before Abraham was, I am" (John 8:58).

The same present tense of the words "I am" is used when God spoke to Moses from the burning bush in Exodus 3:14, where God calls himself "I AM THAT I AM."

What comfort is this doctrine to us? God is in control of every detail of life. Nothing escapes His notice. This is a comfort to God's children, and a dreadful truth for unbelievers.

Questions:
1. Are you God's child? Does it make you happy that God controls everything?
2. Are you not God's child? What are you doing about this serious problem?

Lesson Seven

12. Does God ever change?
No. He is always the same.

"But thou art the same, and thy years shall have no end" (Psalm 102:27).

"For I am the LORD, I change not" (Malachi 3:6a).

Objective: To teach the children that God does not change.

The story of Balaam and Balak (Numbers 22 - 24) might be a good one to use here. King Balak kept hoping that Balaam would curse the Israelites, and Balaam kept trying different locations with the same desire, but God remained steadfast, and would not let Balaam curse His people.

This truth is a comfort for God's children, and for those who seek him. God has promised salvation and deliverance to those who seek and serve him, and he will not change his mind about that. He will not let any harm come to his people, even though they sin. God is faithful!

It is also a warning. God will not change his mind about punishing those who do not love and obey him.

Questions:
1. Can you think of some reasons you are glad God doesn't change?
2. What has God promised to little children who seek him early? (Remember: God doesn't change his mind about his promises!)

Lesson Eight

13. Does God know everything?
Yes. Nothing can be hidden from him.

"Shall not God search this out? for he knoweth the secrets of the heart" (Psalm 44:21).

<u>Objective</u>: To teach the children that God knows everything.

The story of Herod and the wise men (Matthew 2) illustrates this lesson well. The wise men seemed to believe that Herod indeed meant to worship the Baby Jesus. But God, who knows the secrets of the heart, instructed the wise men to go home another way.

Another possibility is to tell the story of the man let down through the roof (Mark 2). Jesus healed him and forgave him his sins, and "perceived in his spirit" (verse 8) that the scribes thought Jesus was speaking blasphemy. He knew their thoughts before they said anything out loud.

The story of Jonah fits beautifully here too. Jonah tried to run away from God, but he was unsuccessful because no one can run away from God.

One more story which illustrates God's omniscience is that of Ananias and Sapphira (Acts 5). The Lord revealed to Peter what this couple's plan was. Nothing is hid from the Lord.

<u>Questions</u>:
1. How does it help you that God knows everything?
2. Why is it foolish to lie to God? Do you ever tell a lie? What should you do if you've told a lie?

Lesson Nine

14. Can God do everything?
Yes. He can do everything that pleases him.

"Who hath directed the Spirit of the LORD, or being his counsellor hath taught him?" (Isaiah 40:13).

Job 42:2a: "I know that thou canst do every thing."; Psalm 115:3: "But our God is in the heavens: he hath done whatsoever he hath pleased."; Luke 1:37: "For with God nothing shall be impossible."

Objective: To teach that God is almighty.

There are many stories to choose from for this lesson. I will list a few of them: multiplying the loaves (Matthew 14); walking on the water (Matthew 14); turning water into wine (John 2);

The story of Jonah (the book of Jonah) - perhaps you want to continue the story if you used it in the last lesson - the fish swallowed Jonah; Elijah at the brook Cherith (1 Kings 17); a handful of flour and a little oil (1 Kings 17).

Many modern "Bible scholars" question these stories. Perhaps you want to talk about the fact that many educated people scoff at these stories. If we believe the whole Bible, however, we are wiser than these scholars.

Questions:
1. How does it help you to know that God can do everything?
2. Who is the only one who can save you?
3. Why is it wise to believe the whole Bible?

23

Lesson Ten

15. Can you see God?
No. I cannot see God but he always sees me.

"Who is the image of the invisible God, the firstborn of every creature" (Colossians 1:15).

"Thou God seest me" (Genesis 16:13).

<u>Objective</u>: To teach the children that although God is invisible, he can see us at all times.

The story of Hagar in the wilderness (Genesis 16) is a nice one to use with this lesson. Hagar left Sarai and fled with her son Ishmael. She thought they would die in the desert. But God saw them and told Hagar where to find water. She did not see God nor the well, but God saw her and provided for her and her son.

The story of Job is also a very appropriate story to tell. Job did not understand why all those calamities befell him, but God's eye was upon him, and he worked all things for Job's good.

Many of the experiences of the Israelites in the wilderness could be used here too. How often the Israelites doubted God! They shouted at Moses, complained, and even turned to idols. But God saw them all the time. He punished them in order to turn them back to himself. He provided for their needs when they called out to him.

<u>Questions</u>:
1. Do you ever forget that God sees you all the time?
2. Why is it a good thing that God sees us all the time?
3. How is it a warning that God sees us all the time?

Lesson Eleven

16. How many Gods are there?
There is only one God.

"I am the LORD, and there is none else, there is no God beside me" (Isaiah 45:5a).

"Hear, O Israel: The LORD our God is one LORD"(Deuteronomy 6:4).

<u>Objective</u>: To teach the children that there is only one God.

For this lesson you could tell one of the many stories in the Bible which show that God was stronger than any of the heathen idols. One clear proof of this truth is the story of the fall of Jericho (Joshua 6). None of the gods of the Canaanites, nor the strength of their warriors was able to stand against the power of the only true God.

Another story you could use is the account of the ark of the covenant being taken by the Philistines (1 Samuel 4, 5, 6). The Philistines thought they had captured God and rejoiced that their god, Dagon, seemed to be stronger than Israel's God. But God showed his almighty power by physically breaking down this idol, and by sending sores to the Philistines.

Another story that shows that God is the one true God, is God's anger with Jeroboam (1 Kings 12 and 13) for setting up altars in Dan and Bethel. Jeroboam's intention was to blend the service of God with idolatry.

Questions:
1. Are there ways in which you do not honour God as you should?
2. How do you know there is only one God?

Lesson Twelve

17. How many persons are there in the one God?
Three persons.

"Go ye therefore, and teach all nations, baptizing them in the name of the Father, and of the Son, and of the Holy Ghost" *(Matthew 28:19).*

18. Who are these three persons?
The Father, the Son, and the Holy Spirit.

"Go ye therefore, and teach all nations, baptizing them in the name of the Father, and of the Son, and of the Holy Ghost" *(Matthew 28:19).*

Objective: To teach the children that God is one God but three Persons.

This is quite a challenging lesson for little ones! Keep it simple. Don't try to explain it, we *cannot* explain this. Perhaps the best approach is to talk about how each Person in the Trinity works together with the others. The story of Jesus' baptism (Matthew 3; Mark 1; Luke 3; John 1) involves each of the three Persons. It is probably best to focus on the story itself. Describe what each of the three Persons did, but don't get into too much doctrine - it will be too hard for small children.

Questions:
1. Do we need to understand everything about God before we may receive a new heart?
2. Does this great God care about little children? What does he do for you?

CREATION (Questions 19-30)

Lesson Thirteen

19. Who made the world?
God.

"And God saw every thing that he had made, and, behold, it was very good" (Genesis 1:31a).

20. Did God make the world out of something?
No. There was nothing else before the world.

"Through faith we understand that the worlds were framed by the word of God, so that things which are seen were not made of things which do appear" (Hebrews 11:3).

21. How did God make the world?
By speaking powerful words.

"Let them praise the name of the LORD: for he commanded, and they were created" (Psalm 148:5).

<u>Objective</u>: To teach that God made the world out of nothing.

This lesson will be a review of Lesson Two, if you told the story of creation then. That is just fine - most children love the story of the creation. Perhaps you could bring in a different worksheet for the children, or a picture for them to colour. Maybe this time you could focus more on the amazing truth that God made the world *out of nothing*.

By way of introduction, ask the children to think of something they've made. You might want to ask them what they used to make it. Then ask if it's possible for them to make something if you don't give them any materials. Ask them if they can make something just by speaking. Of course, they will think that is silly, but direct their attention to the fact that that is just what God did! Nothing is too hard for God. He can give us a clean heart too, if we ask Him.

Questions:
1. Why should we praise God?
2. Aren't you glad this great God wants little children to belong to him?

Lesson Fourteen

22. How long did it take? (i.e. the creation of the world)
Six days.
Genesis 1:1-31

"And God saw everything that he had made, and, behold, it was very good. And the evening and the morning were the sixth day" (Genesis 1:31).

23. What did God do on the seventh day?
He rested and made the seventh day of the week his special day.

"And on the seventh day God ended his work which he had made; and he rested on the seventh day from all his work which he had made" (Genesis 2:2).

<u>Objective</u>: To teach the children that the seventh day is the Lord's day.

There are several aspects to keeping the sabbath day holy. One is the "negative" angle, which is abstaining from work. To illustrate this, you could tell about the children of Israel who were commanded not to gather manna on the sabbath day, and what happened to those who did not listen (Exodus 16).

The "positive" angle is what we *should* do on the sabbath, and there are many stories to choose from here. You could tell about any of Jesus' sabbath miracles, showing that we may do good on the sabbath, for example, the man with the withered hand healed (Matthew 12; Mark 3; Luke

6) and the woman healed of her infirmity (Luke 13). Or, you could tell about the apostle Paul preaching to Lydia (Acts 16) on the sabbath.

The most important thing to stress is that God has graciously set aside a day for us to worship Him and to seek Him. The sabbath day was never meant to be a burden but a joy.

Questions:
1. Why did God give us the sabbath day?
2. Do you look forward to the Lord's Day?

Lesson Fifteen

24. Who was the first man God made?
Adam.

"Male and female created he them; and blessed them, and called their name Adam, in the day when they were created" (Genesis 5:2).

25. What did God make Adam from?
The dust of the ground.

"And the LORD God formed man of the dust of the ground. . ." (Genesis 2:7a).

<u>Objective</u>: To teach the children that God made Adam from dust.

The obvious choice of a story here would be the creation of Adam (Genesis 2). By way of introduction, you could have the children move their hands, their arms, their legs, blink their eyes, etc. Ask how they did that. Point out to them what a marvelous creation our body is. Scientists and doctors have studied for years and years, and still they don't know everything about the human body. Talk about what an amazing thought it is that God formed each of us. He cares for us. We must take good care of the bodies God has created.

<u>Questions</u>:
1. Why do you think some people do not believe that God made us?
2. How do we know that God cares for each of us?

Lesson Sixteen

26. Who was the first woman God made?
Eve.

"And Adam called his wife's name Eve; because she was the mother of all living" (Genesis 3:20).

27. What did God make Eve from?
One of Adam's ribs.

"And the rib, which the LORD God had taken from man, made he a woman, and brought her unto the man" (Genesis 2:22).

<u>Objective</u>: To teach the children that Eve was made by God from one of Adam's ribs.

Tell the story of how God made Eve (Genesis 2). He made Eve to be a helper for Adam. God saw that Adam needed a wife to be his friend. Adam and Eve were the first family.

<u>Questions</u>:
1. Why did God make Eve for Adam?
2. What do you think made Adam and Eve happiest in the garden?
3. What kinds of friends should we choose?
4. Should we pray about our friends? Should we pray for a God-fearing husband or wife?

Lesson Seventeen

28. What did God give to Adam and Eve as well as bodies?
He gave them souls that would never die.

"And the LORD God formed man of the dust of the ground, and breathed into his nostrils the breath of life; and man became a living soul" (Genesis 2:7).

Objective: To teach the children that God gave souls to Adam and Eve that would live forever.

Talk about how the Lord gave Adam a soul (Genesis 2). God separated people from the animals by breathing a soul into Adam. You could bring in the words "image of God" in this lesson, but don't delve too deeply into this mystery. You could talk about the differences between human beings and animals, and what happens when people die, and when animals die.

Questions:
1. What is the difference between people and animals?
2. What will happen to us after we die?

Lesson Eighteen

29. Do you have a soul as well as a body?
Yes. I have a soul that will never die.

"For what is a man profited, if he shall gain the whole world, and lose his own soul? or what shall a man give in exchange for his soul?" (Matthew 16:26).

30. How do you know that you have a soul?
Because God tells me so in the Bible.

"The LORD shall preserve thee from all evil: he shall preserve thy soul" (Psalm 121:7).

<u>Objective</u>: To teach the children that each of us has a soul that must be prepared for eternity.

This lesson is more personal than the previous one, as it takes the truth presented in Lesson Seventeen and now addresses the needs of our own soul.

There are several stories you could tell with this lesson. One story you could tell is the parable of the Rich Fool (Luke 12). This parable ties in nicely with Matthew 16:26 (Question 29). The rich fool made many preparations for this life, but none for eternity.

Another parable you could tell is the one about Lazarus and the Rich Man (Luke 16) where a vivid contrast is made between earthly riches and heavenly treasure.

The parable of the Ten Virgins (Matthew 25) teaches us that we must prepare for eternity, and not neglect our souls.

Questions:
1. Do you think about your soul?
2. Do you ask the Lord for a new heart that loves Him best of all and seeks to walk in His ways?
3. Do you think you should wait until you are older to pray for a new heart? What does the Bible teach us to do?

Lesson Nineteen

31. Were Adam and Eve good when God made them?
Yes, very good. All that God made was good.

"And God saw every thing that he had made, and, behold, it was very good" (Genesis 1:31a).

32. What is sin?
Sin is disobeying or not keeping God's law.

"Wherefore, as by one man sin entered into the world, and death by sin; and so death passed upon all men, for that all have sinned" (Romans 5:12).

"Whosoever committeth sin transgresseth also the law: for sin is the transgression of the law" (1 John 3:4).

Objective: To teach the children that sin is disobedience to God.

Start the lesson by talking about the beauty and perfection of God's creation (Genesis 1, 2). There was no sin. After the fall, sin spoiled everything. Now, every person sins. The Bible is full of stories of people who sinned against God. Some repented; others did not.

You could tell the story of the children who mocked Elisha (2 Kings 2). You can bring this close to their consciences, for who among us has not at one time mocked or teased someone else?

Achan (Joshua 7) is an example of someone who sinned and was punished for it. Exodus 32 tells us of the Israelites' sin of idolatry in worshipping the golden calf. Numbers 20 gives an account of Moses' sin in striking the rock in anger, rather than speaking to it.

Sin always brings grief and sorrow, even though sometimes it may bring pleasure for a time. By nature we are sinful, and want to sin against God. We need to be washed in the blood of Jesus Christ so that we hate sin and flee from it.

Questions:
1. Do you feel happy or sad when you have sinned?
2. Do you confess your sin to God and ask him to wash you in Jesus' blood? What will happen if we don't confess our sins to God?

Lesson Twenty

33. What is *disobeying* God's law?
Doing what God says not to do.

"And the Lord turned, and looked upon Peter. And Peter remembered the word of the Lord, how he had said unto him, Before the cock crow, thou shalt deny me thrice" (Luke 22:61).

"But if ye will not obey the voice of the LORD, but rebel against the commandment of the LORD, then shall the hand of the LORD be against you, as it was against your fathers" (1 Samuel 12:15).

Objective: To teach the children that disobedience is actually rebellion against God, and has sad consequences.

A story that deals with disobedience is the fall in Paradise (Genesis 3), although you will be telling this story in Lesson Twenty One. Adam and Eve blatantly disobeyed God's clearly stated rule: "Of the tree of the knowledge of good and evil, thou shalt not eat of it" (Genesis 2:17a).

The story of Lot's wife (Genesis 19) would fit in with this lesson. She disobeyed God by looking back and became a pillar of salt. In this case, there was no time for repentance, and the consequences of her disobedience were eternal and physical death.

When Moses hit the rock (Numbers 20) rather than speaking to it, he disobeyed the Lord, and for that reason was not allowed to enter Canaan.

King Uzziah, or Azariah, king of Judah (2 Kings

41

15; 2 Chronicles 26) disobeyed the Lord when he took on the duties of a priest. He became proud and thought he should be allowed to do what God had forbidden. His punishment was leprosy.

Disobedience will be punished in God's time. Sometimes the punishment is immediate, and sometimes it seems God takes no notice. But God is just and does all things perfectly, in his time and in the best way.

Questions:
1. Are you sad when you have disobeyed God? Are you sad because you have grieved God, or only because you were punished?
2. What should you do about your sins?
3. Do you ask the Lord every day to make you able and willing to obey him?

Lesson Twenty-One

34. What is *not keeping* God's law?
Not being or doing what God requires.

"And by chance there came down a certain priest that way: and when he saw him, he passed by on the other side" (Luke 10:31)

"Therefore to him that knoweth to do good, and doeth it not, to him it is sin" (James 4:17).

<u>Objective</u>: To teach the children that *not* doing what God wants us to do is also sin, and has consequences.

The parable of the Good Samaritan (Luke 10) fits beautifully with this lesson. The Lord Jesus gives several examples of reactions different people had to the injured man. The priest and the Levite ignored him, while the despised Samaritan helped. The implication is that the priest and the Levite did not gain God's favour by their behaviour in spite of their outward piety.

The parable of the rich man and Lazarus (Luke 16) is similar in this respect. The rich man should have helped poor Lazarus, but neglected him. His end was hell. Perhaps the parable of the barren fig tree (Luke 13) could be used here too. We are like trees, which ought to bring forth good fruit. If we do not seek the Lord, we do not produce good fruit, and are like the fig tree in the parable. Eventually the tree was cut down and burned.

<u>Questions</u>:
1. Do you do what God wants you to do?
2. What is the most important thing we must do?

Lesson Twenty-Two

35. Did Adam and Eve continue to be good?
No. They sinned by disobeying God.

"But of the fruit of the tree which is in the midst of the garden, God hath said, Ye shall not eat of it, neither shall ye touch it, lest ye die" (Genesis 3:3).

36. How did Adam and Eve sin?
By eating fruit that God had said not to eat.

"And when the woman saw that the tree was good for food, and that it was pleasant to the eyes, and a tree to be desired to make one wise, she took of the fruit thereof, and did eat, and gave also unto her husband with her; and he did eat" (Genesis 3:6).

WHAT HAPPENED BECAUSE OF SIN? (Questions 37-42)

37. What happened to Adam and Eve when they sinned?
They were separated from God.

"So he drove out the man; and he placed at the east of the garden of Eden Cherubims, and a flaming sword which turned every way, to keep the way of the tree of life" (Genesis 3:24).

Objective: To teach the children the story of the fall of mankind.

Tell the tragic story of the fall (Genesis 3). Often children think that if they had been in the Garden of Eden, they would not have been so foolish as to listen to the snake. But ask them some questions about obedience to their parents and teachers. Try to get them to understand that we are no better than Adam and Eve.

Questions:
1. Are we any better than Adam and Eve? How do you know this?
2. Can we obey God perfectly?
3. What do we need in order to be able to obey God?

Lesson Twenty-Three

38. Does Adam's sin affect us?
Yes. We are all Adam's children. He acted for us all and as a result we are all born in a sinful condition.

"Wherefore, as by one man sin entered into the world, and death by sin; and so death passed upon all men, for that all have sinned" (Romans 5:12).

39. What name do we give to this sinful condition?
Original sin.

"But I see another law in my members, warring against the law of my mind, and bringing me into captivity to the law of sin which is in my members" (Romans 7:23).

Objective: To teach the children that we were all born in sin (*original* sin).

This is a difficult concept to teach young children. Perhaps the best way is to talk about the truth that we are all born with a sinful heart, and to illustrate it by way of a story.

Cain was the first baby born into the world. Adam and Eve probably thought he was the promised Messiah, but they were so sad to see that he too had been corrupted by sin. The first murder was committed by this first child (Genesis 4). He had godly parents. There were few "evil influences" surrounding him like we have today. But he had sin within.

We are no better than Cain. Ask the children what their thoughts, words, and actions are like when they are angry. Only God's restraining grace keeps us from physically committing murder.

Questions:
1. Are we really as wicked as Cain?
2. Why are we not all murderers?
3. Do you pray for God's grace every day?

Lesson Twenty-Four

40. What other sin are we guilty of as well as original sin?
Actual sin in what we do, say, and think.

"For out of the heart proceed evil thoughts, murders, adulteries, fornications, thefts, false witness, blasphemies" (Matthew 15:19).

Objective: To teach the children that *actual* sins are sins of actions, words, and thoughts.

The story of the tower of Babel could be used for this lesson (Genesis 11). Their thoughts (vs 6), their words (vs 4), and their deeds (vs 5) were wicked. This was especially sad because the Lord had destroyed the entire world with the flood not long before this (Genesis 6-8) because "God saw that the wickedness of man was great in the earth, and that every imagination of the thoughts of his heart was only evil continually" (Genesis 6:5).

Questions:
1. Do you confess your sins to the Lord?
2. Why is it important to confess our sins to God?

Lesson Twenty-Five

41. What does every sin deserve?
God's anger and punishment.

"But your iniquities have separated between you and your God, and your sins have hid his face from you, that he will not hear" (Isaiah 59:2).
"And I will punish the world for their evil, and the wicked for their iniquity" (Isaiah 13:11a).

42. Can anyone go to heaven with this sinful condition?
No. Our hearts must be changed before we can be fit for heaven.

"The wicked shall be turned into hell, and all the nations that forget God" (Psalm 9:17).

<u>Objective</u>: To teach the children that we deserve God's wrath because of our sins.

A story that clearly shows that God punishes sin, is when the children of Israel were bitten with poisonous serpents (Numbers 21) because they "spoke against God, and against Moses" (vs 5). Many people died but it was a just punishment.

Another story you could tell is about the golden calf (Exodus 32). Their punishment was that they had to drink the ground up gold of the calf, and then the Levites killed many of the people who had worshipped the golden calf.

Bring home to the children the fact that we are no better. It is easy to tell ourselves that we

49

would never do such awful things. But how often do we complain when things don't go our way? Or how quickly do we forget God and love other things more than the Lord?

Questions:
1. Are we better than people who don't go to church or read God's Word? Why not?
2. Do you love God best of all? Why does he deserve our love?

SALVATION (Questions 43-57)

Lesson Twenty-Six

43. What did God do to save his people from his anger and punishment?
He sent his Son so that whoever believes in him would not perish but have everlasting life.

"For God so loved the world, that he gave his only begotten Son, that whosoever believeth in him should not perish, but have everlasting life" (John 3:16).

44. Who is God's Son?
The Lord Jesus Christ.

"And the angel answered and said unto her, The Holy Ghost shall come upon thee, and the power of the Highest shall overshadow thee: therefore also that holy thing which shall be born of thee shall be called the Son of God" (Luke 1:35).

Objective: To teach the children that God has provided a way to be saved in Jesus Christ.

If you used the story of the poisonous snakes in the last lesson, you could refresh the children's memories and talk about the brass serpent that Moses was instructed to make (Numbers 21). Talk about the similarities between this brass serpent and the Lord Jesus Christ who died on the cross to redeem his people (Matthew 27; Mark 15; Luke 23; John 19).

You could tell the story of Barabbas (Matthew 27; Mark 15; Luke 23; John 18). Jesus died in the place of this wicked man. In the same way, Jesus takes the place of all his people who deserve only death and hell.

Questions:
1. Has the Lord Jesus taken *your* place?
2. Do you ask the Lord to wash away *your* sins too?

Lesson Twenty-Seven

45. How did he come to this world?
He was born in Bethlehem in a stable.

"And Joseph also went up from Galilee, out of the city of Nazareth, into Judæa, unto the city of David, which is called Bethlehem; (because he was of the house and lineage of David;). . . And she brought forth her firstborn son, and wrapped him in swaddling clothes, and laid him in a manger; because there was no room for them in the inn" (Luke 2:4 and 7).

46. Who was his mother?
The virgin Mary.

"Now the birth of Jesus Christ was on this wise: When as his mother Mary was espoused to Joseph, before they came together, she was found with child of the Holy Ghost" (Matthew 1:18).

<u>Objective</u>: To teach the children about the birth of the Saviour, Jesus Christ.

It's probably best to spread out the story of the birth of Jesus (Matthew 1, 2; Luke 1, 2) over this lesson and the next one. Lesson 28 deals with the fact that Jesus had no earthly father, and this lesson talks about the actual birth of Jesus. The doctrines covered in Lessons 27 and 28 are far beyond the understanding of little children, so it would be best to simply tell the wonderful story of the birth of Christ.

In this lesson you could talk about the angel's appearance to Mary (Matthew 1), and Jesus' birth in a stable because there was no room in the inn (Luke 2). Point out the various ways in which we crowd out Christ, and the critical importance of having room made in our hearts and lives for the Saviour. Mention some ways that we can take our responsibilities seriously by taking time to pray and read the Bible and other good books.

Questions:
1. Why was Jesus born in a stable and not in a palace?
2. Is there room in *your* heart for Jesus?

Lesson Twenty-Eight

47. Did he have an earthly father?
No. He came into the world by the power of the Holy Spirit.

"Now the birth of Jesus Christ was on this wise: When as his mother Mary was espoused to Joseph, before they came together, she was found with child of the Holy Ghost" (Matthew 1:18).

48. Why did he come in this way?
So that he would be free from original sin.

"For such an high priest became us, who is holy, harmless, undefiled, separate from sinners, and made higher than the heavens" (Hebrews 7:26).

<u>Objective</u>: To teach the children that Jesus' Father is God so that he could remain sinless.

As you continue the telling of the birth of Jesus and the events surrounding it, emphasize that Christ is sinless and that he is the King and Saviour of his people. The shepherds made haste to worship him (Luke 2) and told others about him. Simeon and Anna (Luke 2) both recognized him as the long-awaited Messiah, and rejoiced. Simeon called Jesus God's "salvation" (Luke 2:30). He knew that this Child was the Saviour who had come to pay for his sins.

Questions:
1. Is Jesus *your* Saviour? If he is, how do you know? If he is not, what are you doing about it?
2. Are you glad that Jesus is God, so that he can wash away your sin?

Lesson Twenty-Nine

49. Did Jesus ever commit any sin?
No. He obeyed God perfectly always.

"For we have not an high priest which cannot be touched with the feeling of our infirmities; but was in all points tempted like as we are, yet without sin" (Hebrews 4:15).

Objective: To teach the children that Jesus never committed any sin.

A good story to use would be the temptation of Jesus in the wilderness (Matthew 4; Mark 1; Luke 4). Jesus was tempted three times by Satan, but did not yield. Whenever we are tempted to do wrong, we must flee from sin to Jesus Christ. We need the Holy Spirit to live in us to show us our sin, and to make us aware of the sin around us. It is only through Christ's perfect obedience that sinners can be made righteous.

Questions:
1. Why is it so hard for us to fight against sin?
2. What do you do when you realize you've done something wrong?

Lesson Thirty

50. Why was God's Son given the name Jesus?
Jesus means Saviour and he saves his people from their sins.

"And she shall bring forth a son, and thou shalt call his name JESUS: for he shall save his people from their sins" (Matthew 1:21).

<u>Objective</u>: **To teach the children that it is Jesus alone who can save his people from their sins.**

The next few lessons deal with the suffering and death of the Lord Jesus. Since there are many events surrounding the death of Christ, it is a good to spend several lessons on these things. Perhaps in this lesson, which stresses that Christ alone can save us from our sins, you could talk about the tragic spiritual blindness of the religious rulers of the Jews in their condemnation of the Lamb of God (Matthew 26, 27; Mark 14; Luke 22; John 18). They trusted in religion and a strict adherence to the laws of Moses as well as their own additional rules. But they were blind to the beauty of the Saviour God sent. If you like, you can tell one of the stories of Jesus healing the blind (Matthew 9; Matthew 20; Mark 8; Mark 10; John 9).

Tell the children that they must surrender their hearts to Jesus. Urge them to go to him, confessing their sins, and asking for forgiveness, believing that he will save them because of his own promises.

Questions:
1. Do you believe that Jesus is willing and able to save you?
2. Do you believe that there is nothing good in you?
3. Do you believe that only the Lord Jesus Christ can save you?

Lesson Thirty-One

51. How did Jesus save his people from their sin?
Jesus Christ suffered and died in the place of his people to pay the price for all their sins.

"So Christ was once offered to bear the sins of many" (Hebrews 9:28a).

Objective: To teach the children that Jesus suffered in the place of his people.

In this lesson you could tell the story of Peter's denial of Christ (Matthew 26; Mark 14; Luke 22; John 18). Peter, the disciple who so self-confidently boasted that he would never leave Jesus (Matthew 26:33; Mark 14:29; Luke 22:33), denied Jesus as he suffered. Peter deserved to be suffering and dying, but it was the innocent, loving Saviour who bled and died. Peter did not deserve to be forgiven, but the Lord is merciful, and forgave Peter.

Tell the children that the Lord Jesus is willing and able to save them too. Speak of the advantages of belonging to Jesus from their early years. Point them to Christ and His promises.

Questions:
1. Do you love the Lord Jesus?
2. Do you want to serve him all your life? Why is it best to serve the Lord when you are young?
3. Will you be happy or sad if you are God's child?

Lesson Thirty-Two

52. For whom did Jesus Christ suffer and die?
For all the people that God the Father gave him.

"No man can come to me, except the Father which hath sent me draw him: and I will raise him up at the last day. It is written in the prophets, And they shall be all taught of God. Every man therefore that hath heard, and hath learned of the Father, cometh unto me" (John 6:44, 45).

Objective: To teach the children that Jesus suffered and died for those whom the Father has chosen.

In this lesson, you can contrast the reactions to the Lord Jesus at his death (Matthew 26, 27; Mark 14, 15; Luke 22, 23; John 18, 19). The Jews and their leaders cried, "Crucify Him". Pilate was impressed with Jesus and even said that He was innocent, yet he allowed him to be crucified. Herod wanted Jesus to entertain him and was disappointed. These people rejected Christ as their Saviour. What do *you* think of Christ?

God has his chosen people, however. The centurion who stood at the cross believed that Jesus is the Son of God (Matthew 27:54; Mark 15:39; Luke 23:47). The women stood at the foot of the cross because they loved Jesus (Matthew 27:55-56; Mark 15:40, 41; Luke 23:49; John 19:25). The disciples, although they fled and forsook their Master (Matthew 26:56; Mark 14:50), were his children.

Urge the children not to neglect this gracious Saviour, who gave his life so that we might have life. God does not choose people because *they* are good, but because *he* is good.

Questions:
1. Does it make you sad that sin has such sad results?
2. Do you love the Lord Jesus who suffered and died for his people even though he was innocent?

Lesson Thirty-Three

53. Who will be saved?
Only those who repent of their sins and believe in Jesus Christ.

"The time is fulfilled, and the kingdom of God is at hand: repent ye, and believe the gospel" (Mark 1:15).

<u>Objective</u>: To teach the children that those who repent and believe in Christ will be saved.

The story of the thief on the cross (Luke 23:39 - 43) is a beautiful example of sin, repentance, and forgiveness. Salvation is not complicated. We must repent and believe. Talk to the children about their responsibility in repentance and confession of sin. They must put their trust in Jesus for salvation, and for all their daily needs.

<u>Questions</u>:
1. Do you repent of your sin? Why must we repent?
2. Do you trust in the Lord Jesus Christ for everything?

Lesson Thirty-Four

**54. What does to repent of your sin mean?
I am truly sorry for my sins. I hate them
and want to stop doing them. I want to
please God.**

*"Wash you, make you clean; put away the
evil of your doings from before mine eyes;
cease to do evil; learn to do well; seek
judgment, relieve the oppressed, judge the
fatherless, plead for the widow" (Isaiah
1:16, 17).*

<u>Objective</u>: To teach the children that repentance
is turning from sin to God.

There are many stories of repentance in the
Bible. Some are examples of real repentance, and
some show a sorrow because of the consequences
of sin.

You could contrast Peter's repentance (Matthew
26:75; Mark 14:72; Luke 22:62) with that of
Judas (Matthew 27: 3 - 5; Acts 1:18). Peter not
only wept bitterly, but served the Lord boldly for
the rest of his life. Judas was sorry for his act of
betrayal, but did not go to Jesus for forgiveness.
Ask the children what others can tell by observing
their actions. When they sin, what is their
reaction?

<u>Questions</u>:
1. Are you sorry for your sins? What do you do
about your sins?
2. Do you hate sin and want to stop sinning?
3. Do you want to live to please God?

Lesson Thirty-Five

55. Can you decide to repent and believe In Jesus on your own?
No. I can only do so with the help of the Holy Spirit.

"Or despisest thou the riches of his goodness and forbearance and longsuffering; not knowing that the goodness of God leadeth thee to repentance?" (Romans 2:4).

"For the letter killeth, but the spirit giveth life" (2 Corinthians 3:6b).

"And when he is come, he will reprove the world of sin, and of righteousness, and of judgment" (John 16:8).

56. How can you get the Holy Spirit's help?
By praying to God to give me his help.

"If ye then, being evil, know how to give good gifts unto your children: how much more shall your heavenly Father give the Holy Spirit to them that ask him?" (Luke 11:13).

<u>Objective</u>: To teach the children that repentance is the work of the Holy Spirit.

There are several powerful accounts of remarkable conversions in the Bible. You could use any one of these to show that repentance and salvation are God's gift. We do not earn salvation, nor do we deserve it.

The story of Manasseh (2 Kings 21; 2 Chronicles 33) clearly shows that salvation is not given to people who deserve it. Some New Testament stories include Zaccheus (Luke 19), the parable of the prodigal son (Luke 15), and the publican in the temple (Luke 18). In these stories we see the gracious work of the Spirit, giving life to his people.

Questions:
1. Does the Holy Spirit live in your heart?
2. Do you realize your need of the Holy Spirit? Why do we need the Holy Spirit?

Lesson Thirty-Six

57. How were people saved who lived before Christ died?
They believed in the Saviour that God would send.

"For what saith the scripture? Abraham believed God, and it was counted unto him for righteousness" (Romans 4:3).

Objective: To teach the children that God's people are saved by faith in Jesus Christ, before or after his birth.

For this lesson you will, of course, want to use an Old Testament story. The story of Abraham, his faith in God, though it was sorely tried, and his obedience, beautifully illustrates that "faith is the substance of things hoped for, the evidence of things not seen" (Hebrews 11:1). The story of Isaac about to be offered on the altar (Genesis 22) would be a good story to use, because the ram caught in the thicket was the substitute for Isaac, just as Jesus is the Substitute for his people. You could talk about the Old Testament sacrifices, and the feast of the Passover. The continual offerings and sacrifices pointed to the Lamb of God.

Another beautiful illustration of Christ's substitution is the last of the ten plagues in Egypt, which initiated the celebration of the Passover feast (Exodus 11, 12). Only the people who had wiped blood on their doorposts escaped death. They were safe behind the blood. The Israelites knew that one day the Messiah would come, and he would be the Lamb of God.

Questions:
1. Are you glad that Jesus came to pay for sin?
2. Do you hate sin because of what it cost Jesus?

JESUS AS PROPHET, PRIEST AND KING (QUESTIONS 58-61)

Lesson Thirty-Seven

58. In what different ways did Jesus fulfill Old Testament promises about himself?
He came to be a prophet, a priest, and a king.

"For Moses truly said unto the fathers, A prophet shall the Lord your God raise up unto you of your brethren, like unto me" *(Acts 3:22a).*

"As he saith also in another place, Thou art a priest for ever after the order of Melchisedec" *(Hebrews 5:6).*

"Yet have I set my king upon my holy hill of Zion" *(Psalm 2:6).*

<u>Objective</u>: To teach the children about the offices of prophet, priest, and king.

As the next few lessons deal more specifically with the offices of Christ, it might be a good idea to use this lesson to teach the children what each office involves. Perhaps you will want to give them pictures of what a prophet, a priest, and a king would have looked like in Bible times. Talk about each office, and give an example of each. For instance, Elijah was a prophet. What was his work, or calling? Aaron was a priest. What were his duties? David was king of Israel. What did he do all day long? This will help to give the children a much clearer idea of what Christ does in his various offices.

Questions:
1. What does a prophet do?
2. What does a priest do?
3. What does a king do?

Lesson Thirty-Eight

59. How is Christ our prophet?
He teaches us the will of God.

"Howbeit when he, the Spirit of truth, is come, he will guide you into all truth: for he shall not speak of himself; but whatsoever he shall hear, that shall he speak: and he will shew you things to come" (John 16:13).

"For I came down from heaven, not to do mine own will, but the will of him that sent me. And this is the Father's wlll which hath sent me, that of all which he hath given me I should lose nothing, but should raise it up again at the last day" (John 6:38, 39).

Objective: To teach the children that Christ is our prophet by teaching us God's will.

Any of the parables Jesus told would fit into this lesson, since each parable had a "moral" or lesson that Jesus was trying to teach the people. The parable of the Good Samaritan (Luke 10), for example, teaches us about loving our neighbour. The parable of the Good Shepherd seeking the lost sheep (Matthew 18; Luke 15) teaches us that Jesus came to seek and to save the lost. The parable of the unforgiving servant (Matthew 18) teaches us that we must forgive others or we will not find forgiveness with God. Each time Jesus spoke to the people, he was teaching them the will of God.

Questions:
1. Do you want to learn more about God? How can we learn more about God?
2. Are you glad that Jesus is a prophet, so that we can know God's will?

Lesson Thirty-Nine

60. How is Christ our priest?
We are guilty of sin and he has died as a sacrifice for the sins of his people. Now that he has risen and ascended, he continually prays for them.

"And, having made peace through the blood of his cross, by him to reconcile all things unto himself; by him, I say, whether they be things in earth, or things in heaven" (Colossians 1:20).

"But he, being full of the Holy Ghost, looked up stedfastly into heaven, and saw the glory of God, and Jesus standing on the right hand of God" (Acts 7:55).

<u>Objective</u>: To teach the children that Christ is priest by paying for the sins of his people and by praying for them in heaven.

This lesson covers the passion and death of Christ, which we covered in previous lessons. It might be appropriate to now tell the story of Christ's resurrection (Matthew 28; Mark 16; Luke 24; John 20) and ascension (Mark 16:19; Luke 24:50-51 Acts 1). Jesus upholds His people by praying for them continually. What a comfort this is for God's people! Tell the children they may ask Jesus to pray for them, for the Father always hears the prayers of His Son.

Questions:
1. Why is Jesus praying in heaven? For whom is he praying?
2. Are you glad that Jesus is praying at the right hand of the Father?
3. Have you ever asked Jesus to pray for you too?

Lesson Forty

61. How is Christ our King?
He rules the world and defends his people from Satan, the evil one.

"Casting down imaginations, and every high thing that exalteth itself against the knowledge of God, and bringing into captivity every thought to the obedience of Christ" (2 Corinthians 10:5).

"These shall make war with the Lamb, and the Lamb shall overcome them: for he is Lord of lords, and King of kings" (Revelation 17:14a).

<u>Objective</u>: To teach the children that Christ is King, having power over everyone and everything, and defending His people.

The Bible is full of stories of God protecting His people. The plagues of Egypt (Exodus 7 - 12), and the awesome deliverance of the Israelites through the Red Sea (Exodus 14) are excellent illustrations of the Almighty God defending His people. The story of Gideon (Judges 6 - 8) is another example of God's almighty power. When things seem humanly impossible, God can still do wonders. Those who trust in God to help them will never be disappointed.

<u>Questions</u>:
1. Is Jesus your King?
2. Has Jesus ever helped you? Did you thank him for that?

THE TEN COMMANDMENTS
(Questions 62-66)

Lesson Forty-One

62. How many commandments did God give on Mount Sinai?
Ten commandments.

"And God spake all these words, saying, I am the LORD thy God, which have brought thee out of the land of Egypt, out of the house of bondage.

Thou shalt have no other gods before me.

Thou shalt not make unto thee any graven image, or any likeness of any thing that is in heaven above, or that is in the earth beneath, or that is in the water under the earth: thou shalt not bow down thyself to them, nor serve them: for I the LORD thy God am a jealous God, visiting the iniquity of the fathers upon the children unto the third and fourth generation of them that hate me; and shewing mercy unto thousands of them that love me, and keep my commandments.

Thou shalt not take the name of the LORD thy God in vain; for the LORD will not hold him guiltless that taketh his name in vain.

Remember the sabbath day, to keep it holy. Six days shalt thou labour, and do all thy work: but the seventh day is the sabbath of the LORD thy God: in it thou shalt not do any work, thou, nor thy son, nor thy daughter, thy manservant, nor thy maidservant, nor thy cattle, nor thy stranger that is within thy gates: for in six days the LORD made heaven and earth, the sea, and all that in them is, and rested the seventh day: wherefore the LORD blessed the sabbath day, and hallowed it.

Honour thy father and thy mother: that thy days may be long upon the land which the LORD thy God giveth thee.

Thou shalt not kill.

Thou shalt not commit adultery.

Thou shalt not steal.

Thou shalt not bear false witness against thy neighbour.

Thou shalt not covet thy neighbour's house, thou shalt not covet thy neighbour's wife, nor his manservant, nor his maidservant, nor his ox, nor his ass, nor any thing that is thy neighbour's" (Exodus 20:1 - 17).

63. What do the commandments 1-4 tell us?
How to love God.

"Thou shalt have no other gods before me. Thou shalt not make unto thee any graven image, or any likeness of any thing that is in heaven above, or that is in the earth beneath, or that is in the water under the earth: thou shalt not bow down thyself to them, nor serve them: for I the LORD thy God am a jealous God, visiting the iniquity of the fathers upon the children unto the third and fourth generation of them that hate me; and shewing mercy unto thousands of them that love me, and keep my

commandments.
Thou shalt not take the name of the LORD thy God in vain; for the LORD will not hold him guiltless that taketh his name in vain.
Remember the sabbath day, to keep it holy. Six days shalt thou labour, and do all thy work: but the seventh day is the sabbath of the LORD thy God: in it thou shalt not do any work, thou, nor thy son, nor thy daughter, thy manservant, nor thy maidservant, nor thy cattle, nor thy stranger that is within thy gates: for in six days the LORD made heaven and earth, the sea, and all that in them is, and rested the seventh day: wherefore the LORD blessed the sabbath day, and hallowed it" (Exodus 20:3-11).

<u>Objective</u>: To teach the children that the first four commandments instruct us to love God.

The commandments that Israel was guilty of breaking time after time were the first two. It seemed they never learned that their idolatry would be punished. No sooner had Moses gone up Mount Sinai after the giving of the Law, than the Israelites built a golden calf to worship (Exodus 32). Jeroboam set up golden calves in Dan and Bethel (1 Kings 12). Jehu destroyed many priests and worshippers of Baal (2 Kings 10). Balaam was not successful in cursing the Israelites, but his plan to get the Israelites to worship idols worked (Numbers 25 and 31:16). Elijah challenged the Israelites on Mount Carmel as to who was the true God (1 Kings 18). Manasseh led the people in idolatry and wickedness (2 Kings 21; 2 Chronicles 33). Daniel's three friends refused to bow before

Nebuchadnezzar's god, and were cast into the fiery furnace (Daniel 3). Daniel was thrown into the den of lions because he prayed only to God (Daniel 6).

Talk to the children about ways in which we are guilty of breaking these commandments. Whenever we value anyone or anything more than God, we are guilty. God must have the first place in our hearts.

Questions:
1. Do you love God best of all?
2. Can another god give you happiness? Why not?

Lesson Forty-Two

64. What do the commandments 5 - 10 tell us?
How to love others.

"Honour thy father and thy mother: that thy days may be long upon the land which the LORD thy God giveth thee.
Thou shalt not kill.
Thou shalt not commit adultery.
Thou shalt not steal.
Thou shalt not bear false witness against thy neighbour.
Thou shalt not covet thy neighbour's house, thou shalt not covet thy neighbour's wife, nor his manservant, nor his maidservant, nor his ox, nor his ass, nor any thing that is thy neighbour's" (Exodus 20: 12-17).

<u>Objective</u>: To teach that we must love one another.

There are many stories to choose from for this lesson. A nice story in the Old Testament which shows unconditional love is David's kindness to Mephibosheth (2 Samuel 9). Jesus himself is love revealed to us in the flesh. The fact that the Father sent him to earth to pay for the sins of his people is love undeserved. His unending love to a sinful people is clear when Jesus washed the disciples' feet after they had just argued about who of them was the greatest (John 13). Point out to the children the great love of God in Christ Jesus. When he redeems his people, they are loved and show love to others. It is only through Christ that love is restored.

<u>Questions</u>:
1. Do you love God? Why should we love him?
2. Do you love others? Can you think of ways to show that love?

Lesson Forty-Three

65. What is the summary of the ten commandments?

To love the Lord our God with all our heart, and soul, and strength, and mind, and to love our neighbour as we love ourselves.

"Jesus said unto him, Thou shalt love the Lord thy God with all thy heart, and with all thy soul, and with all thy mind. This is the first and great commandment. And the second is like unto it, Thou shalt love thy neighbour as thyself. On these two commandments hang all the law and the prophets" (Matthew 22:37-40).

Objective: To teach the children that we must love God above all, and our neighbour as ourselves.

For this lesson, you could use the parable which Jesus Himself used. "Therefore whosoever heareth these sayings of mine, and doeth them I will liken him unto a wise man, which built his house upon a rock" (Matthew 7:24; also Luke 6:47). Those who do not obey Jesus' words are like a house built on the sand.

Paul was someone who loved God above all, and his neighbour as himself. You could speak in general terms about Paul's missionary travels, or you could choose an incident in his life which showed love to God and others. The story of Paul and Silas and the Philippian jailer (Acts 16) is a fitting story for this lesson. Paul and Silas had been beaten (love to God-suffering for Christ's sake). After the earthquake, instead of fleeing, they preached the gospel to the jailer, showing him God's love.

Questions:
1. Are you building a house on the rock or on the sand?
2. Do you think Paul and Silas are sorry that they suffered so much? Why not?

Lesson Forty-Four

66. Who is our neighbour?
Every human being.

"Which now of these three, thinkest thou, was neighbour unto him that fell among the thieves?" (Luke 10:36).

Objective: To teach the children that every person is our neighbour.

The most obvious choice of a story for this lesson is the parable of the Good Samaritan (Luke 10), which Jesus Himself used to explain who our neighbour is. You may want to use the story of Joseph who reflected Christ when he repaid good for evil (Genesis 45). David spared Saul's life in the cave when he had an opportunity to kill him (1 Samuel 24). Neither Joseph's brothers nor Saul deserved loving treatment, but the love of God in Joseph and in David made them loving in turn.

Questions:
1. Are you a kind and loving person?
2. Can we be truly loving without God's love in our hearts? Why not?
3. How can we receive God's love in our hearts?

Lesson Forty-Five

67. What is the first commandment?
The first commandment is, "Thou shalt have no other gods before me" (Exodus 20:3).

"Unto thee it was shewed, that thou mightest know that the LORD he is God; there is none else beside him" (Deuteronomy 4:35).

68. What does the first commandment teach us?
To worship God only.

"And thou, Solomon my son, know thou the God of thy father, and serve him with a perfect heart and with a willing mind: for the LORD searcheth all hearts, and understandeth all the imaginations of the thoughts: if thou seek him, he will be found of thee; but if thou forsake him, he will cast thee off for ever" (1 Chronicles 28:9).

Objective: To teach that we must worship God only.

Idolatry was a sin the Israelites were guilty of time and again. This was the topic of Lesson 11. Here are the list of stories that you can use: The golden calf (Exodus 32); Jeroboam and the golden calves (1 Kings 12, 13); Jehu destroyed priests and worshippers of Baal (2 Kings 10); Balaam's plan (Numbers 25 and 31:16); Elijah on Mount Carmel (1 Kings 18); Manasseh (2 Kings 21; 2 Chronicles 33); Daniel's three friends (Daniel 3); Daniel in the lions' den (Daniel 6).

It is only in serving the one true God that we find happiness.

<u>Questions</u>:
1. Do people still worship idols today?
2. Why can we not be happy unless we worship God alone?
3. Do you serve God with your whole heart?

THE SECOND COMMANDMENT
(Questions 69-70)

Lesson Forty-Six

69. What is the second commandment?
The second commandment is "Thou shalt not make unto thee any graven image, or any likeness of any thing that is in heaven above, or that is in the earth beneath, or that is in the water under the earth: thou shalt not bow down thyself to them, nor serve them: for I the LORD thy God am a jealous God, visiting the iniquity of the fathers upon the children unto the third and fourth generation of them that hate me; and shewing mercy unto thousands of them that love me, and keep my commandments" (Exodus 20: 4-6).

"Thou shalt make thee no molten gods" (Exodus 34:17).

70. What does the second commandment tell us to do?
To worship God in the way that he tells us in his word, and not to use man-made idols or statues.

"What thing soever I command you, observe to do it: thou shalt not add thereto, nor diminish from it" (Deuteronomy 12:32).

<u>Objective</u>: To teach the children that we may not use images to worship God.

When Josiah became king, he cleansed the temple (2 Kings 22 - 24; 2 Chronicles 34). Obviously there had been a mixture of religions. The Lord will not tolerate his house to be defiled with idolatry. We see this in the New Testament too, when Jesus overturned the tables in the temple (Matthew 21; Mark 11; Luke 19; John 2).

Questions:
1. Why is it wrong to use images to worship God?
2. Do you have things which you love better than God?

THE THIRD COMMANDMENT
(Questions 71-72)

Lesson Forty-Seven

71. What is the third commandment?
The third commandment is, "Thou shalt not take the name of the LORD thy God in vain; for the LORD will not hold him guiltless that taketh his name in vain" (Exodus 20:7).

"And ye shall not swear by my name falsely, neither shalt thou profane the name of thy God: I am the LORD" (Leviticus 19:12).

72. What does the third commandment tell us to do?
To honour God's name and not to use God's name in a careless way.

"Give unto the LORD the glory due unto his name" (Psalm 29:2a).

Objective: To teach the children to honour God's name.

The story of the young man who cursed God (Leviticus 24) shows how serious this sin is. The punishment was death.

Another story is found in 2 Chronicles 32. Sennacherib king of Assyria wrote a letter to King Hezekiah. In this letter Sennacherib belittled God. Hezekiah's response was one of childlike trust: he "prayed and cried to heaven" (verse 20).

The Lord's response is a wonderful example of

his willingness to help, and to defend his Name and his honour! This lesson contains a warning and a comfort. The Lord is jealous of his honour. he will punish those who speak against him, and he will bless and help those who trust in him.

Questions:
1. Do you ever speak against God?
2. Can we speak against God by our actions? How?

THE FOURTH COMMANDMENT
(Questions 73-76)

Lesson Forty-Eight

73. What is the fourth commandment?
The fourth commandment is, "Remember the sabbath day, to keep it holy. Six days shalt thou labour, and do all thy work: but the seventh day is the sabbath of the LORD thy God: in it thou shalt not do any work, thou, nor thy son, nor thy daughter, thy manservant, nor thy maidservant, nor thy cattle, nor thy stranger that is within thy gates: for in six days the LORD made heaven and earth, the sea, and all that in them is, and rested the seventh day: wherefore the LORD blessed the sabbath day, and hallowed it" (Exodus 20:8 - 11).

"Six days thou shalt work, but on the seventh day thou shalt rest: in earing time and in harvest thou shalt rest" (Exodus 34:21).

74. What does the fourth commandment tell us?
To keep the Sabbath day holy.

"Ye shall keep my sabbaths, and reverence my sanctuary: I am the LORD" (Leviticus 19:30; 26:2).

Objective: To teach the children to keep the sabbath day holy.

The story of the man who gathered sticks on the sabbath (Numbers 15) is solemn. His punishment was death by stoning. Nehemiah was angry when he saw people working on the sabbath (Nehemiah 13). He courageously told them they were forbidden to work on the Lord's day. Don't give the children a detailed list of things they are not permitted to do on the sabbath. Families differ on this issue. Be general. Refer to things we may and must do, such as read our Bibles and other good books, sing, pray, go to church, visit the elderly, do good things for others, etc. (This is discussed again in the next lesson.) It is a day the Lord has set aside for us to worship him. It is his gift to us.

Questions:
1. Why did God give us the sabbath day?
2. What should we do on the sabbath day?

Lesson Forty-Nine

75. What day of the week is the Christian sabbath?
The first day of the week or Lord's Day on which Christ rose from the dead.

"And upon the first day of the week, when the disciples came together to break bread, Paul preached unto them" (Acts 20:7a).

"I was in the Spirit on the Lord's day" (Revelation 1:10a).

76. What should we do on the Sabbath?
We should worship God with his people and on our own, pray to him, praise him, read or listen to his word and do good to other people.

"If thou turn away thy foot from the sabbath, from doing thy pleasure on my holy day; and call the sabbath a delight, the holy of the LORD, honourable; and shalt honour him, not doing thine own ways, nor finding thine own pleasure, nor speaking thine own words: then shalt thou delight thyself in the LORD; and I will cause thee to ride upon the high places of the earth, and feed thee with the heritage of Jacob thy father: for the mouth of the LORD hath spoken it" (Isaiah 58: 13, 14).

Objective: To teach the children that we must worship the Lord on the first day of the week.

For this lesson it would be fitting to tell the stories of Jesus' appearances to his disciples on the first day of the week, after his resurrection. He appeared to the disciples (Luke 24; John 20), and to Mary Magdalene, and the other women (Matthew 28; Mark 16). Jesus did show himself to others, but it does not specify that it was on the first day of the week in those instances.

The reference text given for question 76 may be too long for the little ones to memorize, but at least discuss the rich promises given by God to those who will honour his day.

Questions:
1. Should the sabbath be an unpleasant day?
2. Why is it really the best day of the week?

THE FIFTH COMMANDMENT
(Questions 77-78)

Lesson Fifty

77. What is the fifth commandment?
The fifth commandment is, "Honour thy father and thy mother: that thy days may be long upon the land which the LORD thy God giveth thee" (Exodus 20:12).

"Children, obey your parents in the Lord: for this is right" (Ephesians 6:1).

78. What does the fifth commandment tell us to do?
To love and obey our parents and all people in authority over us.

"Children, obey your parents in all things: for this is well pleasing unto the Lord" (Colossians 3:20).

<u>Objective</u>: To teach the children the importance of honouring and obeying their parents, and those in authority over them.

Jesus himself was, of course, the perfect model of obedience. He obeyed his heavenly Father, as well as his earthly parents.

You could tell the story of Jesus in the temple (Luke 2). Jesus would have loved to remain in Jerusalem, learning and studying the scriptures, but he obeyed His parents "and was subject unto them" (verse 51). Later he honoured and showed love to his mother Mary by providing a home for her with John (John 19:25 - 27).

Make the connection between our earthly parents and our heavenly Father. God provided us with families in order to teach us to love and obey him. Sometimes our fathers and mothers sin. Some children have no father or mother. Some children have abusive parents. But God is the perfect Father who will never disappoint those who trust in him.

Questions:
1. Do we have to obey our parents even when we don't feel like it?
2. When is the only time we must disobey our parents or those in authority over us?
3. In what way is God the perfect Father?

THE SIXTH COMMANDMENT
(Questions 79-80)

Lesson Fifty-One

79. What is the sixth commandment?
The sixth commandment is, "Thou shalt not kill" (Exodus 20:13).

"Whosoever hateth his brother is a murderer: and ye know that no murderer hath eternal life abiding in him" (1 John 3:15).

80. What does the sixth commandment tell us to do?
Not to hate, fight with, or hurt anyone.

"Defend the poor and fatherless: do justice to the afflicted and needy. Deliver the poor and needy: rid them out of the hand of the wicked" (Psalm 82:3, 4).

Objective: To teach the children that we may not kill, that is, we must be loving and kind to all.

If you have already told the story of Cain's murder of Abel (Genesis 4), there are, sadly, several accounts of murders in God's Word. Moses murdered the Egyptian (Exodus 2); Abimelech killed his brothers (Judges 9:5); Saul commanded Doeg to kill the priests of the Lord (1 Samuel 22); David had Uriah killed (2 Samuel 11, 12); Absalom killed his brother Amnon (2 Samuel 13:28, 29); King Ahab and his wife Jezebel had

Naboth stoned (1 Kings 21); Joash stoned Zechariah the priest (2 Chronicles 24: 20, 21); King Herod killed all the little children in Bethlehem (Matthew 2); John the Baptizer was beheaded (Matthew 14; Mark 6); Stephen was stoned for his faith (Acts 7). Some of the kings of Israel and Judah murdered others and their families to gain the throne.

Talk about the sin of murder. It lives in each of our hearts. Have we never hated anyone? Have we never wished bad things would happen to someone who displeased us? How we need the cleansing blood of Christ every day!

Questions:
1. Are we better than the people in prison who have actually committed murder?
2. Are we also guilty of murder? How?

THE SEVENTH COMMANDMENT
(Questions 81-82)

Lesson Fifty-Two

81. What is the seventh commandment?
The seventh commandment is, "Thou shalt not commit adultery" (Exodus 20:14).

"For God hath not called us unto uncleanness, but unto holiness" (1 Thessalonians 4:7).

82. What does the seventh commandment tell us to do?
To be pure in our thoughts, words, and behaviour.

"Flee also youthful lusts: but follow righteousness, faith, charity, peace, with them that call on the Lord out of a pure heart" (2 Timothy 2:22).

<u>Objective</u>: To teach the children that God requires us to be pure.

You could tell the story of little Samuel (1 Samuel 2, 3) who did not follow in the evil ways of Eli's sons. Joseph refused to sin with Potiphar's wife (Genesis 39). Solomon had many wives, and they led him to worship other gods (1 Kings 11). David had many wives too, and they and their children brought him much sorrow. He wanted Bathsheba for himself, and the result was sin, grief and sorrow resulted (2 Samuel 11).

One sin leads to another. We need God's grace

every day again to cleanse us and to keep us from sin. We need the Holy Spirit to help us flee from sin.

The children are not too young to be taught to pray for a husband or a wife of the Lord's choosing. Abraham sent his servant to choose a wife for Isaac (Genesis 24). This servant had to swear an oath that he would choose a godly woman for Isaac.

Questions:
1. Can we keep ourselves pure? Why not?
2. How can we become pure in God's sight?

THE EIGHTH COMMANDMENT
(Questions 83-84)

Lesson Fifty-Three

83. What is the eighth commandment?
The eighth commandment is, "Thou shalt not steal" (Exodus 20:15).

"Let him that stole steal no more: but rather let him labour, working with his hands the thing which is good, that he may have to give to him that needeth" (Ephesians 4:28).

84. What does the eighth commandment tell us to do?
To be honest and to work hard to look after ourselves and others, and to respect the property of others.

"Recompense to no man evil for evil. Provide things honest in the sight of all men" (Romans 12:17).

<u>Objective</u>: To teach the children that stealing is sin.

A familiar story of theft is Achan's theft from God from the spoil of Jericho (Joshua 7). His punishment was death: he and his family were stoned.

In order to steal Naboth's vineyard, Jezebel had this innocent man killed (1 Kings 21). Sin never brings joy, only bitterness and grief. God's punishment was death (Ahab: 1 Kings 22;

Jezebel: 2 Kings 9).

There are other ways to steal besides literally taking something that doesn't belong to us. We can steal from others when we say mean things about them, taking away their reputation, their self-confidence, and their happiness.

We can steal from God by not using the strength and talents He gives us for His honour and glory. We steal from God when we do not have a new heart. God says, "Give me thine heart" (Proverbs 23:26), but if we disobey this command, we are stealing from God.

Questions:
1. How can we steal from God?
2. If you steal something, will it make you happy?
3. Why is it better to be honest, even if it brings suffering and pain?

THE NINTH COMMANDMENT
(Questions 85-86)

Lesson Fifty-Four

85. What is the ninth commandment?
The ninth commandment is, "Thou shalt not bear false witness against thy neighbour" (Exodus 20:16).

"Lying lips are abomination to the LORD: but they that deal truly are his delight" (Proverbs 12:22).

86. What does the ninth commandment tell us to do?
To tell the truth at all times.

"These are the things that ye shall do; Speak ye every man the truth to his neighbour" (Zechariah 8:16a).

<u>Objective</u>: To teach the children that God wants us to be honest.

If you haven't already used the story of Ananias and Sapphira (Acts 5), you could use it here. Another story you could use is that of Isaac and the blessing that went to Jacob rather than to Esau (Genesis 27). How much grief resulted from those lies! Jacob was himself the recipient of a lie when his sons showed him Joseph's coat dipped in blood (Genesis 37). Gehazi lied to Naaman and to Elisha (2 Kings 5) and was punished with leprosy.

Lying began already in Paradise, with the serpent telling Eve that she and Adam would be as gods (Genesis 3:5). That eventually resulted in the fall of the entire human race. We have a natural tendency to dishonesty and untruthfulness. We even deceive ourselves when we think we will have plenty of time to repent, or that we are not really quite so sinful as the Bible says we are. We need the Holy Spirit to uncover our sinfulness, to show us the truth.

Questions:
1. Why do we need the Holy Spirit to live and work in our hearts?
2. Does telling a lie make you feel happy? Why not?
3. Can we ever hide the truth from God? Why not?

THE TENTH COMMANDMENT
(Questions 87-88)

Lesson Fifty-Five

87. What is the tenth commandment?
The tenth commandment is, "Thou shalt not covet thy neighbour's house, thou shalt not covet thy neighbour's wife, nor his manservant, nor his maidservant, nor his ox, nor his ass, nor any thing that is thy neighbour's" (Exodus 20:17).

"And he said unto them, Take heed; and beware of covetousness: for a man's life consisteth not in the abundance of the things which he possesseth" (Luke 12:15).

88. What does the tenth commandment tell us to do?
To be content with what we have and not to be envious of others.

"And having food and raiment let us be therewith content" (1 Timothy 6:8).

"But godliness with contentment is great gain" (1 Timothy 6:6).

<u>Objective</u>: To teach the children that we must be thankful and content with what we have.

Covetousness is usually connected with other sins. It was this sin which made Laban change Jacob's wages ten times (Genesis 30-31). Achan coveted and then stole (Joshua 7). Balaam coveted riches and honour (Numbers 22) and went against God's wishes. Saul coveted and disobeyed God's commands (1 Samuel 15). Ahab coveted Naboth's vineyard and murdered him (1 Kings 21).

Covetousness can be subtle and difficult to detect. We are selfish creatures by nature, and do not naturally think of others first. When the Lord saves us and makes us new creations, we want to honour and glorify Him above all, and we begin to love our neighbour as ourselves.

Questions:
1. Can we be happy when we are always wishing for bigger and better things?
2. What are some things we *should* covet, or long for? Hint: they are gifts of God.

KEEPING GOD'S LAWS
(Questions 89-91)

Lesson Fifty-Six

89. Can we obey the ten commandments perfectly?
No. We break them every day in thought, word and deed.

"They are all gone aside, they are all together become filthy: there is none that doeth good, no, not one" (Psalm 14:3).

Objective: To teach the children that no one can keep God's law perfectly.

There are several ways to approach this lesson. You could choose to tell a story about a very wicked person in the Bible and then point out to the children that we are no better. For example, Queen Jezebel (1 Kings 16, 19, 21; 2 Kings 9) died a terrible death because of her wickedness, and some of the wicked kings of Israel and Judah led the people in idolatry.

King Saul (1 Samuel 9 - 31) began his reign with humility but had such a tragic end. Judas Iscariot betrayed Jesus (Matthew 10:4; 26; Mark 14; Luke 22; John 12; 18) and hanged himself (Matthew 27: 3 - 7; John 12:6; Acts 1). These are examples of people who slid into destruction as it were.

There were other wicked people who had "happy endings", such as Manasseh (2 Kings 21; 2 Chronicles 33), whose imprisonment was used for his conversion. Rahab (Joshua 2, 6; Hebrews 11:31; James 2:25) rejected her idols and feared the Lord, even becoming part of the family of the Messiah. The woman at the well (John 4) had lived a sinful life, but was saved by the Lord Jesus, as was Mary Magdalene (Matthew 27:56; 28:1; Mark 15:47; 16; Luke 8:2; John 20). These people's histories have been recorded in scripture to teach us that no one is too sinful for God to redeem.

Another approach you could use is to tell a story of a sick, handicapped, or dead person who was restored, as a picture of what we are by nature. This is more abstract, and may be a bit more difficult for the children to grasp, although the stories are simple enough. There are countless examples of Jesus healing people. Lepers were cleansed (Matthew 8; Mark 1; Luke 5; Luke 17), blind eyes were opened (Matthew 9, Mark 8; Matthew 20; Mark 10), and the dead raised to life (Matthew 9; Mark 5; Luke 8; John 11; Luke 7). We are diseased with sin by nature; we are blind to our dangerous plight; we are dead in sin. We need the Holy Spirit to show us our danger, and we need the Lord Jesus to save us.

Questions:
1. Have you ever decided when you woke up in the morning that you wouldn't do any sin that day? How long did it take before you discovered you couldn't keep that promise you made to yourself?
2. Why can we not keep God's law perfectly? What is wrong with us?
3. How can this problem be solved?

Lesson Fifty-Seven

90. Has anyone ever perfectly obeyed the ten commandments?
Only the Lord Jesus Christ, who is God and man in one person, has perfectly obeyed the ten commandments.

"For we have not an high priest which cannot be touched with the feeling of our infirmities; but was in all points tempted like as we are, yet without sin" (Hebrews 4:15).

"Who did no sin, neither was guile found in his mouth" (1 Peter 2:22).

Objective: To teach the children that only Jesus was perfect in His obedience to the law.

If you've already used the story of the temptation of Jesus (Matthew 4; Mark 1; Luke 4), you could use the accounts of Jesus' sufferings in the Garden of Gethsemane (Matthew 26; Mark 14; Luke 22), His voluntary submission to the Jewish leaders, even suffering the anguish of hell for the sins of his people (Matthew 27:46). He not only obeyed all the commandments perfectly, but paid the price of disobedience for his people.

Questions:
1. Why did Jesus suffer and die on the cross?
2. Do you ever thank him for this great gift?
3. Do you ask him every day to wash your sins away?

Lesson Fifty-Eight

91. What do we deserve for breaking the commandments?
God's anger and punishment.

"For the wages of sin is death; but the gift of God is eternal life through Jesus Christ our Lord" (Romans 6:23).

92. How can we escape from God's anger and punishment?
God, in his mercy, has provided the only way of escape through faith in the Lord Jesus Christ for those who repent.

"Testifying both to the Jews, and also to the Greeks, repentance toward God, and faith toward our Lord Jesus Christ" (Acts 20:21).

Objective: To teach the children that although we deserve only God's wrath, yet in his mercy, he has provided a way of salvation through Christ.

For this lesson, you could review the story of the sacrifice of Jesus Christ for the sins of his people. You could perhaps focus on the unworthiness of those he died for. Not only were the Jews and their religious rulers wicked and cruel, but what about the disciples? Hadn't they all told Jesus that they would die with him (Matthew 26:33-35; Mark 14:29-31; Luke 22:33; John 13:37)? But these same disciples argued over who was the greatest just before the Last Supper (Luke 22:24) and didn't think they would betray Jesus; (their question, literally translated, "It's not me, is it?" showed their unwillingness to believe they were capable of doing such an awful thing). They fell asleep in the Garden of Gethsemane when Jesus was agonizing in prayer (Matthew 26; Mark 14; Luke 22), and "forsook him and fled" when he was arrested (Matthew 26:56; Mark 14:50; John 16:32) after foolishly trying to fight for Jesus, cutting off Malchus' ear. How much the disciples must have added to the sufferings of the dear Saviour through their insensitivity and ignorance of Jesus' agony!

Yet for such people the Saviour suffered and died. What a wonder! There is hope for anyone in this precious Redeemer.

Questions:
1. Is anyone too wicked or sinful for Jesus to save?
2. Do you believe you are sinful and need Jesus to save you?
3. Is Jesus willing to save little children too?

THE WAY TO BE SAVED
(Questions 92-94)

Lesson Fifty-Nine

93. What is faith?
Faith in Jesus Christ is a gift from God, when we trust in him completely to save us from sin.

"For God so loved the world, that he gave his only begotten Son, that whosoever believeth in him should not perish, but have everlasting life" (John 3:16).

Objective: To teach the children that faith is God's gift of trusting in Christ to save us from sin.

There are many stories in the New Testament of Jesus healing people of physical ailments, because, sad to say, most people were only interested in the temporal blessings Jesus gave.

Happily, there are accounts of people who came to Jesus and had their sins forgiven also. They knew he was the only one who could forgive their sins, because they believed he is the Son of God.

The palsied man was healed of his sickness, but his sins were forgiven first (Matthew 9; Mark 2; Luke 5).

The woman who washed Jesus' feet was told by Jesus that her sins were forgiven (Luke 7). The man who lay at the pool of Bethesda for 38 years was healed, and was told not to sin anymore (John 5). The woman taken in adultery was forgiven (John 8).

The man born blind was healed, and led to see that Christ is the Son of God, thus he received spiritual sight as well (John 9).

These people trusted in Jesus Christ for their soul's salvation. Faith is trusting Jesus alone for our salvation. Only in him and by his atoning sacrifice can we be saved. Urge the children to go to the Lord Jesus in prayer, trusting him to save them.

Questions:
1. Is Jesus Christ the only way to be saved? Can't we save ourselves by being good? Why not?
2. Have your sins been forgiven?
3. Do you trust in Jesus Christ alone?

Lesson Sixty

94. What is repentance?
Repentance is also a gift from God when we are made truly sorry for our sins and turn from them all to Jesus Christ and live to please him.

"And the publican, standing afar off, would not lift up so much as his eyes unto heaven, but smote upon his breast, saying, God be merciful to me a sinner" (Luke 18:13).

<u>Objective</u>: To teach the children that repentance is turning from sin to God with a desire to please Him.

The parable from which the reference text is taken is the well known story of the publican and the Pharisee (Luke 18). Jesus used this parable to point out the difference between godly humility and sinful pride. The picture of the publican beautifully portrays God-given repentance. He went to God's house with his sorrow for sin - he took his need to God, who showed, by way of the daily sacrifices offered in the temple, his willingness to forgive sin.

Other stories which illustrate true repentance are the Ninevites (Jonah) who repented when Jonah preached to them, Peter (Matthew 26:75; Mark 14:72; Luke 22:62) who wept bitterly after denying Christ, and the prodigal son (Luke 15) who returned to his father and asked for forgiveness.

Questions:
1. Why is sin so terrible?
2. Why must we repent?
3. Will Jesus forgive us if we confess our sins to him?
4. Should we wait until we're older to repent, or should we repent today? Why?

EXPERIENCING GOD'S SALVATION
(Questions 95-96)

Lesson Sixty-One

95. How does God help us to experience his salvation?
By his word the Bible, the sacraments, and prayer.

"And they continued stedfastly in the apostles' doctrine and fellowship, and in breaking of bread, and in prayers" (Acts 2:42).

"And that from a child thou hast known the holy scriptures, which are able to make thee wise unto salvation through faith which is in Christ Jesus" (2 Timothy 3:15).

<u>Objective</u>: To teach that God's Word, the sacraments, and prayer help Christians to live out their salvation.

For this lesson, you could tell the story of Pentecost (Acts 2), and then tie in the reference text, which speaks of the godly life these people lived. By means of the Word of God, the sacraments, and prayer, they learned God's laws and his will, and lived accordingly.

The travellers to Emmaus (Luke 24) finally had their eyes opened after Jesus explained the Bible to them, prayed, and broke bread with them.

When Hezekiah had cleansed the temple, he reinstated the service of the Lord according to

God's laws, prayed to God in the presence of the people, and kept the Passover with the people (2 Chronicles 29-31).

This lifestyle of thanksgiving (sanctified prayer, scripture reading, and use of the sacraments) flows out of repentance and forgiveness.

Questions:
1. Why must we live a life that pleases God?
2. Does pleasing God sometimes mean we must say no to what we want, or to what our friends might be doing?

Lesson Sixty-Two

96. How should we read the Word?
We should read the Bible carefully and believe all of it.

"All scripture is given by inspiration of God, and is profitable for doctrine, for reproof, for correction, for instruction in righteousness" (2 Timothy 3:16).

<u>Objective</u>: To teach the children that God's Word is the truth and must be studied diligently.

Ezra and Nehemiah were prophets who brought about reform in the land of Israel after their captivity in Babylon. They spoke against the evils that they noticed, and taught the people the importance of following God's commandments. There is no true prosperity for those who do not obey God's Word.

<u>Questions</u>:
1. Why is it so important to obey God's Word?
2. Do you believe the whole Bible? Do you read it every day? Ask God to make you love his Word.

BAPTISM AND THE LORD'S SUPPER
(Questions 97-101)

Lesson Sixty-Three

97. What are the sacraments of the church?
The sacraments are Baptism and the Lord's Supper.

"Go ye therefore, and teach all nations, baptizing them in the name of the Father, and of the Son, and of the Holy Ghost: teaching them to observe all things whatsoever I have commanded you: and, lo, I am with you alway, even unto the end of the world. Amen" (Matthew 28:19, 20).

<u>Objective</u>: To teach the children that there are two sacraments: baptism and the Lord's Supper.

Start the lesson by talking about what happens when a person is baptized. Talk about what they see: water is put on the person's forehead, or they may be immersed. Talk about what baptism means. Tell the children what the Lord promises in baptism - perhaps you could even read some sentences from the Form for the Administration of Baptism (*The Psalter*, Eerdmans, 1995, pages 126-130) and explain them. Tell the children they have been set apart because of baptism, and that God is able and willing to save them.

Then talk about what they see in the Lord's Supper: bread and wine. Talk about the fact that people come to the table. Why do they do that? What does it all mean?

Keep the discussion general, not too detailed, or they will not understand. Also, try to make it as personal as you can. What does God have to say to the children through these sacraments?

In the following lessons, each of the sacraments will be studied. Several suggestions for stories are given for each. You could use any one of those for this lesson too.

Questions:
1. What does your baptism mean to you?
2. Do you pray that one day you may attend the Lord's Supper?
3. Why did God give us the sacraments?

Lesson Sixty-Four

98. What is Baptism?

Baptism is the outward sign of washing with water, in the name of the Father, and of the Son, and of the Holy Spirit, which tells us about the cleansing from sin by the blood of Jesus Christ and about belonging to God.

"Now when they heard this, they were pricked in their heart, and said unto Peter and to the rest of the apostles, Men and brethren, what shall we do? Then Peter said unto them, Repent, and be baptized every one of you in the name of Jesus Christ for the remission of sins, and ye shall receive the gift of the Holy Ghost. For the promise is unto you, and to your children, and to all that are afar off, even as many as the Lord our God shall call. And with many other words did he testify and exhort, saying, Save yourselves from this untoward generation. Then they that gladly received his word were baptized: and the same day there were added unto them about three thousand souls" (Acts 2:37 - 41).

Objective: To teach the children that baptism is a sign and a seal of God's promise to wash away all the sins of His people through the blood of Christ.

There are several stories you could tell about people who were baptized. There were the converts in Samaria (Acts 8); the Ethiopian eunuch (Acts 8); Paul (Acts 9); Lydia (Acts 16); the Philippian jailer and his household (Acts 16);

121

the believers in Corinth (Acts 18); Ephesus (Acts 19).

Baptism is not salvation, but it seals God's promise of salvation.

Questions:
1. Does baptism save you? Can people go to heaven without being baptized?
2. What comfort does the Lord give to you in baptism ?

Lesson Sixty-Five

99. What is the Lord's Supper?
The Lord's Supper is the outward sign of eating bread and drinking wine which tells us about the death of the Lord Jesus Christ for his people.

"That the Lord Jesus the same night in which he was betrayed took bread: and when he had given thanks, he brake it, and said, Take, eat: this is my body, which is broken for you: this do in remembrance of me. After the same manner also he took the cup, when he had supped, saying, This cup is the new testament in my blood: this do ye, as oft as ye drink it, in remembrance of me" (1 Corinthians 11:23b-25).

100. What do the bread and wine represent?
The body of Christ and the blood of Christ.

"The cup of blessing which we bless, is it not the communion of the blood of Christ? The bread which we break, is it not the communion of the body of Christ?" (1 Corinthians 10:16).

"And when he had given thanks, he brake it, and said, Take, eat: this is my body, which is broken for you: this do in remembrance of me. After the same manner also he took the cup, when he had supped, saying, This cup is the new testament in my blood: this do ye, as oft as ye drink it, in remembrance of me" (1 Corinthians 11:24, 25).

<u>Objective</u>: To teach the children that the Lord's Supper is a sign and a seal of salvation by way of Christ's broken body and shed blood.

Perhaps you would like to begin this lesson by talking about the Passover (Exodus 12). Talk about the lamb that had to be killed, and how that lamb without blemish pointed to Christ, the spotless Lamb of God. Then tell the story of the Last Supper (Matthew 26; Mark 14; Luke 22). Jesus ate the Passover meal with His disciples, knowing he was the Lamb that would soon die on the cross. Every time the Lord's Supper is celebrated, God's people are commanded to remember the suffering and death of Jesus Christ. His blood washed away their sin, and his broken body bore the wrath of God they deserved.

<u>Questions</u>:
1. Why is it important for us to think about the sufferings and death of Jesus?
2. Does it make you sad that Jesus had to suffer so much because of our sins?
3. Are you happy and thankful that Jesus was willing to do this?

Lesson Sixty-Six

101. Why did Jesus Christ command this sacrament to be kept by those who trust in him?
So that his suffering and death would be remembered and proclaimed till the end of the world.

"For as often as ye eat this bread, and drink this cup, ye do shew the Lord's death till he come" (1 Corinthians 11:26).

<u>Objective</u>: To teach the children that the sacrament of the Lord's Supper is intended to remind us of Christ's death.

If you feel that you've spent enough time on the topic of the sacrament of the Lord's Supper, then you could put this question with the others in the previous lesson, but it would result in a lot of memory work for the children. Finding another story to go with this lesson is a challenge.

You could use the story of the travellers to Emmaus (Luke 24). It was when Jesus broke the bread, that the men recognized Him.

It might be a bit of a stretch, but you could tell the parable of the great supper (Luke 14), or the parable of the man without a wedding garment (Matthew 22). In the first parable, you would talk about the connection between the host of the great supper and God. In the second, you would talk about the connection between the wedding garment and salvation. The Lord's Supper is an imperfect picture of the great feast in heaven. Everyone in heaven will have a "wedding garment", and no place will be empty.

Questions:
1. Why must we celebrate the Lord's Supper often?
2. Do you long to attend the Lord's Supper also?
3. What should you do when the Lord's Supper is being celebrated, even if you may not yet be able to attend because you are not a professing member of the church?

PRAYER (Questions 102-105)

Lesson Sixty-Seven

102. What is prayer?
Prayer is asking God for things that are agreeable to him, confessing our sins to him and thanking him for all his mercies.

"Be careful for nothing; but in every thing by prayer and supplication with thanksgiving let your requests be made known unto God" (Philippians 4:6).

103. In whose name should we pray?
In the name of Jesus Christ.

"Verily, verily, I say unto you, Whatsoever ye shall ask the Father in my name, he will give it you" (John 16:23b).

Objective: To teach the children that prayer is asking God for our needs in Christ's name, with confession and thanksgiving.

There are so many examples in scriptures of answered prayer. Perhaps you would like to make two lessons out of this one, since prayer is such an important topic. It is so important that children learn to take every need, great and small, to the Lord. In forming this habit, they learn dependence upon the Lord. As parents and teachers, we must train them in the way they must go. We must lead them to Jesus. One way of doing this is to teach them to take every detail of their lives to

God in prayer. "In all thy ways acknowledge him, and he shall direct thy paths" (Proverbs 3:6).

Some examples of praying people are: Abraham (Genesis 18) who interceded for Sodom; Moses (Exodus 32) when he pleaded for the undeserving Israelites; Gideon (Judges 6) when he wanted to know God's will for him; Hannah (1 Samuel 1) when she poured out her grief to the Lord, and asked for a child; Samuel (1 Samuel 7) who asked the Lord to help the Israelites in battle; Job, who did not understand what was happening to him; David (Psalms) who led a life of prayer; Solomon (2 Chronicles 6) who prayed at the dedication of the temple; Hezekiah (2 Kings 19) who asked the Lord for help in fighting the enemies; Ezra (Ezra 8) who asked for God's help; Daniel (Daniel 6) who suffered because he prayed; Zacharias (Luke 1).

Although the Lord is very merciful and answers even the prayers of unbelievers, he especially delights to answer the prayers of his people, particularly when they plead in the name of Jesus Christ. Moses was a man who interceded for the people of Israel while focusing on the honour and glory of God and his great Name. Elijah prayed that the people might know the Lord (1 Kings 18) by showing his power on Mount Carmel. Paul's entire ministry was one in which he desired to glorify Christ (1 Corinthians 2:2). Similarly, John the Baptizer said that Christ must increase and he must decrease (John 3:30).

Jesus himself, of course, is the only one who offers perfect prayers. When on earth, he sometimes prayed all night (Luke 6:12), and wrestled in prayer in the Garden of Gethsemane (Matthew 26; Mark 14; Luke 22). Other prayers of Christ can be found in Luke 3:21; 9:29; 23:34; and John 17. Now, at the right hand of his Father, he prays for his people. What a blessed comfort! This will be covered in a later lesson.

Jesus gave so many encouragements to prayer while he was on earth (Matthew 7:7; Luke 11:9; Luke 18:1; John 15:7). Other scripture passages also urge us to pray (1 Chronicles 16:11; Psalm 91:15; Isaiah 55:6; 58:9; 65:24; Jeremiah 33:3; Zechariah 13:9; 1 Thessalonians 5:17 and many others). What a merciful God we serve!

Questions:
1. Why must we pray?
2. Does Jesus like to hear the prayers of little children?
3. Does he like to hear about the details of their everyday lives?
4. Does he promise to answer us when we pray in Jesus' name? (See John 14:13)

Lesson Sixty-Eight

104. What has God given us to teach us to pray?
The whole Bible teaches us about prayer, but Jesus especially teaches us about it in the Lord's Prayer.

105. What is the Lord's Prayer?
The Lord's Prayer is:

"Our Father which art in heaven,
Hallowed be thy name. Thy kingdom come.
Thy will be done in earth, as it is in heaven.
Give us this day our daily bread. And forgive
us our debts, as we forgive our debtors.
And lead us not into temptation, but deliver
us from evil: For thine is the kingdom, and
the power, and the glory, for ever. Amen"
(Matthew 6:9b - 13).

<u>Objective</u>: To teach the children that the Lord Himself has given us a model in the Lord's prayer.

For this lesson, you could go through the Lord's Prayer line by line, explaining what each petition means. In the previous lesson, many examples of praying people were given. You could choose one of those to illustrate one or more petitions. Moses (Exodus 32), Elijah (1 Kings 17, 18) and the other prophets, and Hezekiah (2 Kings 19) wanted to hallow God's Name. Jesus' prayer in the Garden of Gethsemane was concluded with "Nevertheless, not my will, but thine, be done" (Luke 22:42b). The parable of the unforgiving servant (Matthew 18) illustrates the petition "forgive us our debts, as we forgive our debtors."

Do not dismiss the children without having impressed upon them the willingness of the Lord to hear and answer prayers, especially those of children. "If ye then, being evil, know how to give good gifts unto your children, how much more shall your Father which is in heaven give good things to them that ask him?" (Matthew 7:11). It is your task to recommend this precious God and Saviour to the children. "Jesus said, Suffer little children, and forbid them not, to come unto me: for of such is the kingdom of heaven" (Matthew 19:14). "Come, ye children, hearken unto me: I will teach you the fear of the LORD" (Psalm 34:11). Prayer is communication with God. What a miracle that He is willing to communicate with sinful people!

Questions:
1. Why did Jesus give us the Lord's Prayer?
2. Why is it important to pray to God even if he already knows all about us?
3. Do you love to pray?

WHERE IS JESUS NOW?
(Questions 106-108)

Lesson Sixty-Nine

106. Did Christ stay in the grave after he died?
No. He rose from the dead on the third day.

"He is not here: for he is risen, as he said"
(Matthew 28:6a).

<u>Objective</u>: To teach the children that Jesus rose from the dead on the third day.

The obvious choice of a story for this lesson is the resurrection of Jesus Christ. The story of the resurrection includes several "little stories" such as the watchmen who fled (Matthew 28), the women at the tomb (Matthew 28; Mark 16; Luke 24; John 20), Peter and John going to the tomb (Luke 24; John 20), and Mary Magdalene weeping at the tomb (John 20).

<u>Questions</u>:
1. Does it make you happy to know that Jesus is alive today?
2. How does the risen Saviour help you today?

Lesson Seventy

107. Where is Christ now?
He is in heaven, sitting at the right hand of God the Father, praying always for his people.

"So then after the Lord had spoken unto them, he was received up into heaven, and sat on the right hand of God" (Mark 16:19).

Objective: To teach the children that Jesus Christ now sits at the right hand of his Father in heaven, and there he prays continually for his people.

For this lesson, you would tell the story of Christ's ascension into heaven (Mark 16:19; Luke 24:50-51; Acts 1). After you tell the story, talk about what Jesus does in heaven now. It may seem odd to the children that Jesus prays. He is God, so why does he need to pray? Without going into heavy doctrines, explain it along these lines: Christ Jesus and his Father, and the Holy Spirit care so much about God's people, that they talk about them every day. Jesus prays to his Father, asking him to save them and bless and keep them. God's people are like stubborn, wandering sheep. They need constant care. That is why the Lord Jesus prays for them constantly. He loves them and desires to keep them safe. Because he prays for his people, Satan is not able to snatch them away from God.

Questions:
1. Do you ask the Lord Jesus to pray for you?
2. Why does Jesus pray for His children?

Lesson Seventy-One

108. Will he come to the world again?
Yes. At the end of time, Christ will come to judge the world.

"When the Son of man shall come in his glory, and all the holy angels with him, then shall he sit upon the throne of his glory: and before him shall be gathered all nations: and he shall separate them one from another, as a shepherd divideth his sheep from the goats" (Matthew 25:31, 32).

Objective: To teach the children that Christ will come again to judge all people.

Matthew 24 and 25 contain Jesus' warnings about the coming judgment. There are several parables you could choose from to accompany this lesson.

In Matthew 25:1-13 we read the parable of the ten virgins. The message behind this parable is that we must be ready for Christ's return. Later on in the same chapter, Jesus talks about the actual judgment, when He will separate the sheep from the goats (verses 31-46). This is a very solemn chapter, one we must not gloss over. We must not unduly frighten the children, but we must be honest.

Speak truthfully about the coming judgment, but also point the little ones to Christ Jesus, who saves anyone who comes to him. He will not despise anyone who flees to Him for salvation. Use this opportunity to speak about the Saviour, warning them to "flee from the wrath to come" and find refuge in Christ.

<u>Questions</u>:
1. Why must we always be ready to die?
2. Why is it so important to seek the Lord while we are young?

DEATH (Questions 109-110)

Lesson Seventy-Two

109. What happens when a person dies?
The body decays but the soul lives on and goes either to heaven or to hell.

"For if we believe that Jesus died and rose again, even so them also which sleep in Jesus will God bring with him" *(1 Thessalonians 4:14).*

110. Will the bodies of the dead be raised again?
Yes. When Christ returns, the bodies of the dead will be raised and joined to their souls forever.

"So also is the resurrection of the dead. It is sown in corruption; it is raised in incorruption: it is sown in dishonour; it is raised in glory: it is sown in weakness; it is raised in power" *(1 Corinthians 15:42,43).*

Objective: To teach the children that when a person dies, his body decays but will be raised again at the last day, while his soul goes immediately to either heaven or hell.

This is a continuation of the previous lesson. You could tell the parable in Matthew 25:14-30 about the talents given to the servants.

This has some rather complex lessons, but if you keep it simple, the children should catch the main lesson, which is to use our time wisely, and thus be ready when Christ returns. We have been given many gifts: God's Word, a church, a Christian home, godly parents perhaps, faithful ministers and teachers. What are we doing with all these gifts?

Although salvation is by faith through the gracious work of the Holy Spirit, we will be held accountable for all the gifts God has given us. Urge the children to seek the Lord while they are young. Tell them to ask the Lord to save them and bless them. God will never turn away a child who truly seeks Him.

Questions:
1. What gifts has God given you? What does he want you to do with them?
2. Are you using the gifts God has given you? Are you diligently seeking the Lord?

Lesson Seventy-Three

111. Where does God send the wicked?
To hell.
"Then shall he say also unto them on the left hand, Depart from me, ye cursed, into everlasting fire, prepared for the devil and his angels" (Matthew 25:41).

112. What is hell?
A terrible place of torment and punishment.
"For I have five brethren; that he may testify unto them, lest they also come into this place of torment" (Luke 16:28).

Objective: To teach the children that hell is a place of punishment for the ungodly.

If you haven't used the parable of Lazarus and the rich man (Luke 16), it would fit well with this lesson. Although it is a parable, it does portray the torment of those in hell. Jesus talked often about hell with the intent of warning His hearers. He wanted the people to turn from sin to God and be forgiven. In Matthew 23:37-39 and Luke 13:34, 35, we read his lament over Jerusalem. In Luke 19:41 we learn that Jesus wept over the city. What a precious Saviour! What a terrible sin it is to ignore such pleadings!

Questions:
1. Do you ever think about hell? Why do you think Jesus told the people about hell?
2. How can we escape hell?

Lesson Seventy-Four

113. Where does the godly person go at death?
To heaven.

"Then shall the King say unto them on his right hand, Come, ye blessed of my Father, inherit the kingdom prepared for you from the foundation of the world" (Matthew 25:34).

114. What is heaven?
A glorious, joyful place where Christ is.

"And God shall wipe away all tears from their eyes; and there shall be no more death, neither sorrow, nor crying, neither shall there be any more pain: for the former things are passed away" (Revelation 21:4).

<u>Objective</u>: To teach the children that heaven is glorious because Christ is there.

For this lesson you could use especially the book of Revelation to talk about what heaven will be like:
- Christ, the Lamb of God is the focus (Revelation 7:17)
- many people (Revelation 14:1; 19:6)
- joy (Psalm 16:11)
- no more sea (Revelation 21:1)
- no more sorrow or crying or pain or death (Revelation 21:4)

- no curse (Revelation 22:3)
- no night (Revelation 22:5)
- endless glory (2 Timothy 2:10)

Because the children are very young it may be beneficial to use one of Jesus' parables to illustrate these truths. The parable of the great supper (Luke 14) was meant to warn people against neglecting the gospel, but the feast indicates the joy in the presence of God in heaven. It is a wonderful opportunity to point out to the children that the Lord Jesus invites us to Himself, and how rude, sinful, and foolish it would be to turn our backs on Him.

Questions:
1. Do you long to go to heaven? Why?
2. Who is most important in heaven? Why?

Bible Stories Suggested

1. Parable of the two sons (Matthew 21)
    Parable of the houses on the sand and the rock
    (Matthew 7; Luke 6)
2. Creation (Genesis 1)
3. Jeremiah (Jeremiah 36)
    Habakkuk
    John (Revelation 1 - 3; 14)
4. Plagues of Egypt (Exodus 7 - 12)
    Pillar of cloud (Exodus 13)
    Golden Calf (Exodus 32)
    Jericho (Joshua 6)
    David fights the Philistines
    (2 Samuel 5; 1 Chronicles 14)
    Paul stoned (Acts 14)
    Paul bitten by a snake (Acts 28)
5. Centurion's servant healed (Matthew 8)
6. Jews challenging Jesus (John 8)
    Burning bush (Exodus 3)
7. Balaam and Balak (Numbers 22 - 24)
8. Herod and the wise men (Matthew 2)
    Paralytic let down through the roof (Mark 2)
    Jonah
    Ananias and Sapphira (Acts 5)
9. Multiplying the loaves (Matthew 14)
    Walking on the water (Matthew 14)
    Water changed to wine (John 2)
    Jonah, continued
    Elijah at the brook Cherith (1 Kings 17)
    Widow of Zarapheth (1 Kings 17)
10. Hagar (Genesis 16)
    Job
    Israelites journeying through the wilderness
11. Jericho's destruction (Joshua 6)
    Dagon (1 Samuel 4 - 6)
    Jeroboam's altars (1 Kings 12, 13)

12. Baptism of Jesus
    (Matthew 3; Mark 1; Luke 3; John 1)
13. Creation, review (Genesis 1)
14. No manna on the sabbath (Exodus 16)
    Jesus' "sabbath miracles", for example:
    man with the withered hand
    (Matthew 12; Mark 3; Luke 6)
    woman with the infirmity (Luke 13)
    Paul preaching to Lydia (Acts 16)
15. Creation of Adam (Genesis 1, 2)
16. Creation of Eve (Genesis 2)
17. Adam receives a soul (Genesis 2)
18. Rich fool (Luke 12)
    Rich man and Lazarus (Luke 16)
    Ten virgins (Matthew 25)
19. Children who mocked Elisha (2 Kings 2)
    Achan (Joshua 7)
    Golden calf (Exodus 32)
    Moses striking the rock (Numbers 20)
20. The Fall (Genesis 3)
    Lot's wife (Genesis 19)
    Moses striking the rock (Numbers 20)
    King Uzziah, or Azariah (2 Kings 15; 2 Chronicles 26)
21. Parable of the good Samaritan (Luke 10)
    Parable of the rich man and Lazarus (Luke 16)
    Parable of the barren fig tree (Luke 13)
22. The Fall (Genesis 3)
23. Cain (Genesis 4)
24. The tower of Babel (Genesis 11)
    The flood (Genesis 6 - 8)
25. Poisonous serpents (Numbers 21)
    Golden calf (Exodus 32)
26. Poisonous serpents (Numbers 21)
    Barabbas (Matthew 27; Mark 15; Luke 23; John 18)
27. Angel's appearance to Mary (Matthew 1)
    Stable birth of Christ (Luke 2)
28. Shepherds (Luke 2)
    Simeon and Anna (Luke 2)

29. Temptation of Christ (Matthew 4; Mark 1; Luke 4)
30. Jewish leaders condemn Christ
    (Matthew 26, 27; Mark 14; Luke 22; John 18)
    Healing of the blind
    (Matthew 9; Mark 8; John 9; Matthew 20; Mark 10)
31. Peter's denial
    (Matthew 26; Mark 14; Luke 22; John 18)
32. Jews' rejection of Christ
    (Matthew 27; Mark 15; Luke 23; John 18)
33. Thief on the cross (Luke 23)
34. Peter's repentance (Matthew 26; Mark 14; Luke 22)
    Judas' remorse/death (Matthew 27; Acts 1)
35. Manasseh (2 Kings 21; 2 Chronicles 33)
    Zaccheus (Luke 19)
    Parable of the prodigal son (Luke 15)
    Parable of the publican in the temple (Luke 18)
36. Abraham offering Isaac (Genesis 22)
    Passover (Exodus 11, 12)
37. Discussion of prophet priest and king, using Elijah,
    Aaron, and David as examples
38. Parable of the good Samaritan (Luke 10)
    Parable of the lost sheep (Matthew 18; Luke 15)
    Parable of the unforgiving servant (Matthew 18)
39. Christ's resurrection
    (Matthew 28; Mark 16; Luke 24; John 20)
    Ascension (Mark 16:19; Luke 24:50-51; Acts 1)
40. Plagues of Egypt (Exodus 7 - 12)
    Red Sea crossing (Exodus 14)
    Gideon (Judges 6 - 8)
41. Golden calf (Exodus 32)
    Jeroboam and the golden calves (1 Kings 12)
    Jehu destroyed priests and worshippers of Baal
    (2 Kings 10)
    Balaam's plan (Numbers 25; 31:16)
    Elijah on Mount Carmel (1 Kings 18)
    Manasseh (2 Kings 21; 2 Chronicles 33)
    Daniel's three friends (Daniel 3)
    Daniel in the lions' den (Daniel 6)

42. Mephibosheth (2 Samuel 9)
    Jesus washing the disciples' feet after they argued
    (John 13)
43. Parable of the houses built on the sand/rock
    (Matthew 7; Luke 6)
    Paul and Silas and the Philippian jailer (Acts 16)
44. Parable of the good Samaritan (Luke 10)
    Joseph and his brothers (Genesis 45)
    David spares Saul's life (1 Samuel 24)
45. Golden calf (Exodus 32)
    Jeroboam and the golden calves (1 Kings 12)
    Jehu destroyed the priests and worshippers of Baal
    (2 Kings 10)
    Balaam's plan (Numbers 25; 31:16)
    Elijah on Mount Carmel (1 Kings 18)
    Manasseh (2 Kings 21; 2 Chronicles 33)
    Daniel's three friends (Daniel 3)
    Daniel and the lions' den (Daniel 6)
46. Josiah cleans the temple
    (2 Kings 22, 23; 2 Chronicles 34)
    Jesus overturns the tables in the temple (Matthew 21;
    Mark 11; Luke 19; John 2)
47. Young man who cursed God (Leviticus 24)
    Sennacherib's letter to Hezekiah (2 Chronicles 32)
48. Man gathering sticks on the sabbath (Numbers 15)
    Nehemiah angry with the people working on the
    sabbath (Nehemiah 13)
49. Jesus' appearance to the disciples (Luke 24; John 20),
    Jesus appearance to Mary and the women
    (Matthew 28; Mark 16)
50. Jesus in the temple (Luke 2)
    Jesus provides a home for Mary (John 19)
51. Murders committed by:
    Cain (Genesis 4)
    Moses (Exodus 2)
    Abimelech (Judges 9)
    Saul/Doeg (1 Samuel 22)
    David (2 Samuel 11, 12)
    Absalom (2 Samuel 13)

Ahab and Jezebel (1 Kings 21)
Joash (2 Chronicles 24)
Herod - the children in Bethlehem (Matthew 2)
Herod - John the Baptizer (Matthew 14; Mark 6)
The Jews - Stephen (Acts 7)

52. Little Samuel (1 Samuel 2, 3)
Joseph fled from Potiphar's wife (Genesis 39)
David and Bathsheba (2 Samuel 11)
Solomon's wives (1 Kings 11)
Abraham's servant send to find a wife for Isaac
(Genesis 24)

53. Achan (Joshua 7)
Naboth's vineyard (1 Kings 21)

54. Ananias and Sapphira (Acts 5)
Isaac blesses Jacob (Genesis 27)
Joseph's brothers lie to Jacob (Genesis 37)
Gehazi's lies (2 Kings 5)
Lies in Paradise (Genesis 3)

55. Laban and Jacob (Genesis 30)
Achan (Joshua 7)
Balaam (Numbers 22)
Saul's disobedience (1 Samuel 15)
Ahab and Naboth's vineyard (1 Kings 21)

56. Queen Jezebel (1 Kings 16, 19, 21; 2 Kings 9)
Judas Iscariot (Luke 22)
(Matthew 10:4; 26; 27; Mark 14; John 6:70; 12:6; 18)
Manasseh (2 Kings 21; 2 Chronicles 33)
Rahab (Joshua 2, 6; Hebrews 11:31; James 2:25)
King Saul (1 Samuel 9 - 31)
The woman at the well (John 4)
Mary Magdalene (Matthew 27:56; 28:1; Mark 15:47;
16; Luke 8:2; John 20)
Lepers were cleansed
(Matthew 8; Mark 1; Luke 5; Luke 17;)
Blind eyes were opened
(Matthew 9, Mark 8; Matthew 20; Mark 10)
The dead raised to life
(Matthew 9; Mark 5; Luke 8; John 11; Luke 7)

57. The temptation of Christ (Matthew 4; Mark 1; Luke 4)

Garden of Gethsemane
(Matthew 26; Mark 14; Luke 22)
Forsaken of His Father (Matthew 27)

58. Disciples argued over who was greatest before the last supper (Luke 22)
Disciples fled (Matthew 26, Mark 14, John 16)
Disciples slept in the Garden
(Matthew 26; Mark 14; Luke 22)

59. Palsied man (Matthew 9; Mark 2; Luke 5)
Woman washed Jesus' feet (Luke 7)
Man at the Pool of Bethesda (John 5)
Woman taken in adultery (John 8)
Man born blind (John 9)

60. Parable of the publican and the Pharisee (Luke 18)
Ninevites' repentance (Jonah)
Peter's repentance (Matthew 26; Mark 14; Luke 22)
Parable of the prodigal son (Luke 15)

61. Pentecost (Acts 2)
Travellers to Emmaus (Luke 24)
Hezekiah cleanses the temple (2 Chronicles 29 - 31)

62. Ezra
Nehemiah

63.

64. Converts in Samaria baptized (Acts 8)
Ethiopian eunuch (Acts 8)
Paul converted and baptized (Acts 9)
Lydia (Acts 16)
Philippian jailer (Acts 16)
Believers in Corinth (Acts 18)
Believers in Ephesus (Acts 19)

65. Passover (Exodus 12)
Last Supper (Matthew 26; Mark 14; Luke 22)

66. Travellers to Emmaus (Luke 24)
Parable of the great supper (Luke 14)
Parable of the man without a wedding garment
(Matthew 22)

67. Abraham (Genesis 18) Who interceded for Sodom
Moses (Exodus 32) When he pleaded for the undeserving Israelites

Gideon (Judges 6) When he wanted to know God's will for him

Hannah (1 Samuel 1) When she poured out her grief to the Lord, and asked for a child

Samuel (1 Samuel 7) Who asked the Lord to help in battle

Elijah (1 Kings 18) Who asked the Lord to show His power on Mount Carmel

Job - Who did not understand what was happening to him

David (Psalms) Who led a life of prayer

Solomon (2 Chronicles 6) Who prayed at the dedication of the temple

Hezekiah (2 Kings 19) Who asked the Lord for help in fighting the enemies

Ezra (Ezra 8) Who asked for God's help

Daniel (Daniel 6) Who suffered because he prayed

Zacharias (Luke 1) Who prayed for a son

Paul's entire ministry was one in which he desired to glorify Christ (1 Corinthians 2:2)

John the Baptizer said that Christ must increase and he must decrease (John 3:30).

Jesus Himself prayed (Matthew 26; Mark 14; Luke 6:12; Luke 3, 9, 22, 23; John 17)

68. Moses (Exodus 32)
Elijah (1 Kings 17, 18)
Hezekiah (2 Kings 19)
Jesus in the Garden of Gethsemane (Luke 22)
Parable of the unforgiving servant (Matthew 18)

69. Resurrection of Christ
(Matthew 28; Mark 16; Luke 24; John 20)

70. Ascension of Christ (Mark 16; Luke 24; Acts 1)

71. Parable of the ten virgins (Matthew 25)
Sheep and the goats (Matthew 25)

72. Parable of the talents (Matthew 25)

73. Parable of the rich man and Lazarus (Luke 16)

74. Parable of the great supper (Luke 14)

Bible
Questions
and
Answers
for children

A Children's Catechism

by Carine Mackenzie

Using the Authorised King James Version

1. Who made you?
God.
Genesis 1.27.

2. Why did God make you?
To glorify him and enjoy him.
1 Corinthians 10. 31.

Simple one sentence answers in contemporary English language make this catechism one that children will understand and benefit from. These scripture truths and doctrines will remain with them for the rest of their lives.

Train up a child in the way he should go: and when he is old, he will not depart from it.
Proverbs 22:6

Also available from Christian Focus Publications:

The Shorter Catechism
Key Questions and answers
on the Christian Faith
With Scripture proofs and notes
by Roderick Lawson

ISBN: 1-85792-288-3

Exposition of
The Westminster Confession of Faith
Robert Shaw

The Westminster Confession is the most comprehensive doctrinal credal statement of its kind. This classic explanation of the confession provides a thorough theological grounding. "Provides a miniature course in theology," Sinclair Ferguson.

ISBN: 0 906731 046
$24.99/£15.99

BIBLE TIME

A series of Bible stories
for 5-7 year olds
by Carine Mackenzie

Esther, The Brave Queen	ISBN 0 90673 164X
Gideon, Soldier of God	ISBN 0 90673 102X
Hannah, The Mother who Prayed	ISBN 0 90673 1100
John, The Baptist	ISBN 0 90673 1445
Jonah, The Runaway Preacher	ISBN 0 90673 1666
Joshua, The Brave Leader	ISBN 0 90673 1127
Martha and Mary, Friends of Jesus	ISBN 0 90673 1674
Mary, Mother of Jesus	ISBN 0 90673 1062
Nehemiah, Builder for God	ISBN 0 90673 1119
Peter, The Apostle	ISBN 0 90673 1658
Peter, The Fisherman	ISBN 0 90673 1089
Rebekah, The Mother of Twins	ISBN 0 90673 1453
Ruth, The Harvest Girl	ISBN 0 90673 1070
Simon Peter, The Disciple	ISBN 0 90673 1097

BIBLE WISE

A series of Bible stories
for 7-11 year olds
by Carine Mackenzie

Miriam
The Big Sister's Secret   ISBN 1 85792 0988

Samuel
The Boy who Listened   ISBN 1 85792 1992

Jesus is Alive
The Resurrection   ISBN 1 85792 3448

David
The Fearless Fighter   ISBN 1 85792 1984

Joseph
God's Dreamer   ISBN 1 85792 343X

Elijah
God's Miracle Man   ISBN 1 85792 097X

Saul
Miracle on The Road   ISBN 1 85792 2964

Daniel
The Praying Prince   ISBN 1 85792 1550

The Birth of Jesus
The Promised Child   ISBN 1 85792 2972

Sarah and Abraham
The Wonderful Promise   ISBN 1 85792 1569

Diana Kleyn

Diana Kleyn lives in Grand Rapids, Michigan, and is a member of the Heritage Netherlands Reformed Congregation there. She has a Master of Arts in teaching and taught elementary grade school in Jordan Station, Ontario for three years. She is now wife to Chris and mother of Ben, Mark, and Tim.

When her children began attending catechism classes, she realized the need for updated catechism books for the children. Believing that the Lord had laid this matter concerning the souls of the children on her heart, she inquired if there was a way in which she could help with this project. Prayer and providence led to the completion of a catechism booklet and an accompanying teachers' manual.

It is her prayer that the Lord will use the catechism booklet and the Teacher's Manual to help teachers and students discover the riches of God and His Word, and that many children may seek and find the Lord in their youth.

Carine Mackenzie

Carine Mackenzie lives in Inverness, Scotland. The author of many children's books she has been published throughout the world in many languages. Her first book was published when her children were still quite young and she now has the pleasure of reading her stories to her grand-children - Lydia and Esther.

She strongly believes that Bible stories should be retold accurately to children in a way that will help them to become enthusiastic readers of the Bible for themselves, now and later in their lives.

Writing this children's catechism has been both a challenge and a privilege to her. Having learnt the Shorter Catechism herself as a young child she realises the benefit this has been to her Christian life. It has been a hope of hers and others at Christian Focus Publications that *Bible Questions and Answers* as well as *Diana Kleyn's Teachers' Manual* will bring this privilege to another generation and that many young people who discover God's word for themselves will discover their Lord and Saviour Jesus Christ.

Commendations

'Giving our children basic instruction in the faith is one of the primary responsibilities we have as Christian parents. Using this children's catechism is an ideal way of doing this. Here are the essential questions with the single-sentence, easily-remembered answers. This is God-centred, Christ-honouring, life-transforming, character-building teaching - a long term investment in a few pages.'
Sinclair B. Ferguson

'The doctrines of Scripture in contemporary language that is easy to memorize. This book is an effective, foundational tool for godly parents to use in catechizing their children.'
Joel Beeke

'I heartily commend this children's catechism.'
R. C. Sproul

'This new children's catechism is actually quite remarkable. It clearly articulates important doctrines in a manner that is clear yet without any compromising of the essential truths that parents need to teach their children. Sadly, the present generation has virtually lost the older practice of catechizing little ones. This much needed resource could go a long way in correcting this problem by providing a useable and simple tool for serious Christian parents to use.'
John Armstrong

As evangelicals, we have analysed the harmful cultural influences on our children but have been less effective in offering positive solutions to the problem. It is a joy, therefore, to recommend very highly Carine MacKenzie's new catechism for children.

Here is something that Christian parents, grandparents and friends can do for the character development and wholesome spiritual growth of the young generation: teach them this catechism!

It is Biblically sound throughout; a fine and clear summation of the structure of Reformed Theology. It is both comprehensive and comprehensible. Written in very plain and current English, it wastes no words and keeps to the point at issue in each question, and is organized so that theological concepts follow each other in proper order, much like its model, the Westminster Shorter Catechism.

It presents profound truth as simply as possible. As a father of five, I deem it to be happily accessible to children. It conveys a spirit of uplifting devotion.

This catechism could make a great difference in the lives of those who learn it. My prayer is that it may be very widely read.

Douglas F. Kelly, RTS
Charlotte

CHRISTIAN FOCUS

Good books with the real message of hope!

Christian Focus Publications publishes biblically-accurate books for adults and children.

If you are looking for quality Bible teaching for children then we have a wide and excellent range of Bible story books - from board books to teenage fiction, we have it covered.

You can also try our new Bible teaching Syllabus for 3-9 year olds and teaching materials for pre-school children.

These children's books are full of biblical truth, an ideal way, by God's grace, to help children learn to know themselves and Jesus Christ. Our aim is to help children find out about God and get them enthusiastic about reading the Bible, now and later in their lives.

Find us at our web page:
www.christianfocus.com